CYCLETTES

TREE ABRAHAM

The Unnamed Press
Los Angeles, CA

For Abigail—
brains, heart, & courage.

The only rule of travel is,
Don't come back the way you went.
Come a new way . . .
There is no question I am someone starving.
There is no question I am making this journey
to find out what that appetite is.

—Anne Carson, *Plainwater*

A spiral begins at a point and moves onward, not extravagant or lackadaisical like a meander, but smooth and steady, spinning around and around that central point or a single axis . . . A spiraling narrative could be a helix winding downward—into a character's soul, or deep into the past—or it might wind upward, around and around to a future. Near repetitions, but moving onward. What gives a spiraling narrative a sense of ending? Good question, for spirals could go on forever.

—Jane Alison, *Meander, Spiral, Explode*

(1)

On a first grade spelling list is the word *bike*. On a second grade (2)
spelling list is the word *cycle*. We learn first the thing, second our
relationship to it.

> **bike** [informal of **bi·cy·cle** /ˈbaɪsɪk(ə)l/]
> *noun*
>> a vehicle with a frame holding two wheels
>> front wheel is connected to handlebars that steer, that brake
>> back wheel is connected to chains connected to pedals
>> connected to a person—torque

> **cy·cle** /ˈsaɪk(ə)l/
> *noun*
>> 1. a complete series, which might repeat
>> 2. a time period of events/states/interactions that recur
>> in order and duration
>
> *verb*
>> 1. to ride a bicycle (SEE ABOVE)
>> 2. to move in a revolution, often around a central axis
>
> + *–tte*
>> SEE pp.7–207

My earliest encounter with a bicycle that I can claim with any certainty (3)
is not a true memory, but a photo record of me found tucked with other
outtakes behind posed photos in a clear pocket album. Technically,
it is a tricycle. And if you were to judge my childhood based on said
photo, it might appear that I grew up in a trailer park—which is ironic
since a trailer connotes a home that is mobile, and nothing typifies
my childhood less than the suggestion of movement. I am barefoot in
an undershirt and sweats on a rusted trike in a backyard filled with
plastic child things: a potty, an upturned wading pool, a picnic table.
I look determined, though too tiny to pump the pedals. Where would
I have hoped to have gone? I couldn't have known then. It is May 11,
1992, and I am 26.5 months old.

My first bicycle was sparkly magenta with squishy white handlebars (4)
and a coaster brake system. The head tube had a 3-D silver crest of a
mountain motif affixed to it. I rubbed that insignia as if it authenticated
membership into a trailblazer's club.

Buried in the twenty hours of 8mm video cassette footage from the (5)
beginning years of my parents becoming parents is a one minute and
two second clip of me riding the magenta bike with training wheels at
four years old. Mom is filming from the porch, zooming in over the
fence to capture me, trailed by Dad and my sister sauntering on foot
at nearly the same speed that I can manage on wheels. My simpering
face is cocked toward Mom the entire labored pedal down the path. I
stop when perpendicular to the frame, stumble off the bike in a jog to
our backyard fence to wave at Mom. I want her watching me. Watch
me ride a bike. Watch me go on by.

MAY 21, 199

MAY 21 199

MAY. 21. 1994

MAY 21 1994

MAY. 21. 1994

(6)   Sometimes I meet an adult who has never ridden a bicycle. I am left aghast. I cannot comprehend a bicycle-less existence—to not know or want to know a bike ride. There is an ugliness to watching an adult learn to ride a bike, but we all have learning gaps. There are things I missed out on as a child, things my parents didn't model or think to pass along to me. Organizing my adulthood sometimes feels like a series of catch-up sessions to compensate for my parents' oversights (like how to cook, strike a match, apply makeup, pay taxes, camp, dance, celebrate, maintain close friendships, be happy . . .). But I am catching up, and those things absent for much of my life are starting to appear as if they have been part of me all along.

(7)   A friend learned to ride a bike in his mid-twenties. Out of embarrassment, he would practice on his childhood block in the middle of the night. He bikes to work every day now.

(8)   I must have begun riding my magenta bicycle with four wheels that became two, but I do not remember that upgrade. I do remember watching my younger sister ride a training wheel–less bike for the first time. We were in the schoolyard on that kind of field so worn down that its compacted ground with grassy patches looked like a scalp suffering alopecia. As the eldest, I had learned on pavement, but by now Dad had wisened to starting my younger sisters on a softer surface. My sister Daryl[1] was born with a tumor pressing against the left side of her brain (a fact we didn't discover until adulthood) that causes the right side of her body to be slightly paralytic. Motor activities sent her into fits of frustration until she could develop her own workarounds. I held my breath as Daryl mounted her sparkly blue retro bike with a banana seat (undoubtedly a garage sale find). She immediately set off in loops around the field with a lionhearted ease. When I stitch together that moment in my mind, I see myself jumping up and down

and cheering her name in elation. She was championing this thing that was supposed to be hard. I watched her becoming free as if it were an extension of my own freedom.

The balding schoolyard was also the site of bicycle tragedy for my (9) friend Bertie. The story went: she was splayed out at the bottom of the hill when a teenager on a bike came barreling down it and ran right over both her legs. For what seemed like all of first grade, Bertie had two full-length leg casts and was wheeled around the schoolyard by a posse fighting for pushing powers. I wanted injury accoutrement—bandages, crutches, scars. Her casts were crowded with Sharpied doodles consecrating her fandom. *Barney & Friends* usually had a kid actor with a broken arm, often in a neon-pink or mustard-yellow cast, probably caused from falling out of a tree. Kids in the latter half of the twentieth century were always falling out of trees and down wells. I was jealous of the special attention injuries garnered. I was jealous of Bertie even when she was wailing in pain and had to leave class or sit out of activities. While brushing my teeth I would bite down hard on my canker sores to try to simulate the degree of pain she must have felt. I wanted to experience the out of the ordinary, to separate from the mundane masses and do what nobody else got to do.

Once, I strung a skipping rope from the seatpost on my sister's bike (10) to a Hula-Hoop. Rollerblades on, I got inside the hoop and had her ride as fast as she could back and forth on the path behind our house. The limits to our play were either end of that path out back or the parallel extent in front that spanned where our street intersected a busy road on one end and the curve of the court on the other end (165 yards—which Google Maps estimates is one minute of cycling or two minutes of walking). This might have been one of the most dangerous activities I ever instigated as a girl, alongside swing set acrobatics and consecutive lunches at McDonald's. I was never reckless enough to justify injury accoutrement. The closest I came was spraining a thumb, not mid-sport, but sport-adjacent, when it was nicked by a classmate's basketball being thrown back into a bin.

(11) With our limited horizon, sometimes my sisters and I would have slow bike races. While torpor requires poise and micro-movements to keep from tipping over, mostly I won because my resolute adherence to tasks outlasted the spasmodic tendencies of most children. I wasn't about speed as much as flux. Not fast, but thorough and moving, even if sometimes microscopically.

VELOCITY

MODE	AVG. MPH
WALKING	0.15
JOGGING	3–3.5
RUNNING	4–6
SKATEBOARDING	6–15
ROLLERBLADING	8–16
CYCLING—BEGINNER	12
CYCLING—COMMUTER	15–19
CYCLING—ADVANCED	20–24
CYCLING—RACER	25–28

I had longings for a childhood like Vada Sultenfuss's in *My Girl*. I (12)
longed to ride down Main Street through back alleys under tree-lined
sidewalks to the dock beneath the willow, side by side with a best
friend turned boyfriend. Small-town America was always presented as
an idyllic playground for latchkey kids to romp around unsupervised.
My suburbia lacked the charm and amenities of a quaint historic film
locale. The neighborhood was sun-bleached from saplings in lieu of the
forests cleared to build it; services were packaged in box-store oases
surrounded by parking lot deserts; and whatever utopic delusions
once lulled parents into negligence had been obliterated in the wake
of missing kids on milk cartons and sensationalist news coverage of
guns, drugs, and peanut allergies.

I've noticed that time speeds by faster when biking in nature than when (13)
biking in the city. Time speeds by faster when walking in the city than
when walking in nature.

Self-referential encoding—the mentation that marries our environment (14)
with our identity—is made possible through entering *default network
mode*, wherein the body is on autopilot and the brain is at wakeful
rest, lost in daydream and wander. I enter this mode most often when
cycling. The bike becomes a telekinetic apparatus, effortlessly chan-
neling creative epiphanies from the world into my mind.

The farthest I ever habitually veered from home as a child was on (15)
bike rides with my father. Dad towed my sisters in a bike trailer and I
followed on my two-wheeler. I tried to retrace our standard route on a
map of Hunt Club—the network of suburban streets and parks in the
south end of Ottawa, Ontario, Canada, that was encircled by linked
pathways. We rode by my elementary school, which was visible from
my house, onward past familiar backyards of school friends toward
Greenboro Park. I went to a Catholic school. My best friend, who also

lived on my street, went to the public elementary and secondary schools farther on. The only time I saw those schools was on this bike ride. It helped me visualize the setting of her stories. Her schools had the same initials: R.B. One named after a female astronaut and the other after a painter. At the park, we would do all the same things we could have done at the parks by my house, only it felt special because we were somewhere else—two miles away (a twelve-minute ride for an adult). We played on the play structure, which was different, because each

play structure is always slightly different enough to excite a child. We were spun on the tire swing. We attempted baseball, Frisbee, football, or soccer. There was a patch under a tree where four-leaf clovers could be found (I was a wanter of wishes—ladybugs and eyelashes on fingertips, shooting stars, birthday candles, and pennies heads up). There were sprinklers to run through on hot days. Maybe if we were lucky, on the way home we would stop at the Quickie convenience store for a Freezie. Maybe.

(16)   Greenboro Community Centre was where my Brownies ("Girl Scouts" in America) chapter met once a week. In our groups (I was a Nymph), we paid our dues (25 cents) and then . . . made friends? Learned something? Fashioned pizza ovens out of tinfoil . . . mastered knot tying with licorice laces . . . those are my only lasting takeaways. My parents didn't keep us long enough in any one organized activity to reap the benefits of fellowship and praxis. I don't believe I ever earned a badge. I tried embroidering my own.

This one resembles the actual Cycling Merit Badge. To earn it, *Scouting for Girls: The Original 1920 Girl Scout Handbook* states one must:

1.   Own a bicycle, and care for it, cleaning, oiling, and making minor repairs, readjusting chain, bars and seat.

2.   Be able to mend a tire.

3.   Demonstrate the use of a road map.

4.   Demonstrate leading another bicycle while riding.

5.   Know the laws of the road, right of way, lighting and so forth.

6.   Make satisfactory report to Captain of a bicycle Scouting expedition as to the condition of a road with camping site for an overnight hike.

7.   Pledge the bicycle to the government in time of need.[2]

I am far from achieving any of these requirements. But the symbol reminds me of Buddhism's Noble Eightfold Path, which I think I am more likely to achieve in my lifetime.

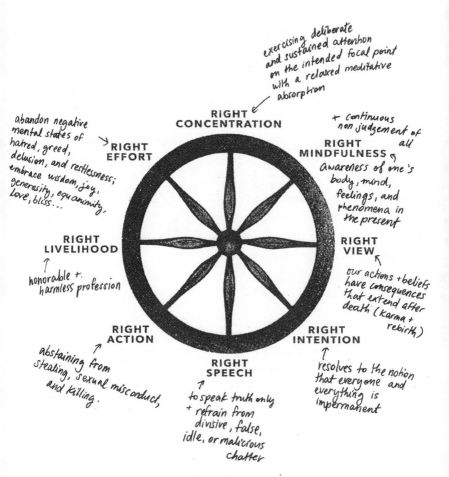

exercising deliberate and sustained attention on the intended focal point with a relaxed meditative absorption

RIGHT CONCENTRATION

+ continuous non judgement of all

RIGHT MINDFULNESS
awareness of one's body, mind, feelings, and phenomena in the present

abandon negative mental states of hatred, greed, delusion, and restlessness; embrace wisdom, joy, generosity, equanimity, love, bliss...

RIGHT EFFORT

RIGHT LIVELIHOOD

honorable + harmless profession

RIGHT VIEW
our actions + beliefs have consequences that extend after death (karma + rebirth)

RIGHT ACTION

abstaining from stealing, sexual misconduct, and killing.

RIGHT SPEECH
to speak truth only + refrain from divisive, false, idle, or malicious chatter

RIGHT INTENTION
resolves to the notion that everyone and everything is impermanent

(17)   On the Canadian television station TVOkids, I watched the British art program *Art Attack*. Each episode included a segment where host Neil Buchanan would gather objects from around town and assemble them in a wide-open area. Spliced aerial shots created suspense as to what the macro-scene would become. Unrelated little pieces were nudged together to make something else, but it didn't make sense until all the pieces were in place and you panned far far back. Once he made a parking lot–sized bicycle. The frame was made of rows of neon-orange traffic cones. A fleet of identical black cars scuttled across the scene like beetles before Maestro Buchanan guided them into two circles simulating spinning rubber bike wheels. I was tickled by the idea that fourteen cars were needed to capture the movement of one bicycle.

(18)   The Ford Model T was "the car that put the world on wheels." The Model T's predecessor, the Ford Quadricycle, was essentially two bicycles put together. Henry Ford invented both. Henry Ford cycled to his automobile factory every day.

(19)   My relationship to cars: I have ridden my bicycle to every DMV appointment.

(20)   Bike shorts were layered beneath my dresses and skirts so cycling wouldn't threaten my girlhood modesty. It wasn't until my early twenties that I shed the underlayer when I realized that no more skin shows while riding a bike than lounging on the beach in a swimsuit and my thighs were sick of being made to feel indecent.

(21)   I used to say I was a *biker*, until I learned it was the colloquial term for someone who rode a motorcycle, particularly one who is part of a motorcycle gang. But to say I am a *cyclist* feels like a colloquialism for members of a more serious cycling culture.

Official cycling clothing has never made it into my wardrobe: fabrics (22)
of stretchy spandex, moisture-wicking, flatseams, sculpted paneling,
padded butt underwear, the sheen of nylon and Lycra, the reflective
highlighter colors. Perhaps that's the divide between those who con-
fidently declare themselves cyclists and those of us who are simply
riders of bikes.

Anyway, I was much more enamored by those who rode bikes. There (23)
was a teen girl on my street whom I would see only when she rode past
our house to hers six houses down. The image I have of her is with
dirty-blond hair in two braids, a crocheted halter top in multicolored
stripes, bellbottom jeans, and a low-slung khaki backpack. She rode
upright, hands-free. The image includes her holding an open book as
she maundered by, but that seems unlikely. I don't think we ever spoke,
but she became my archetype of cool.

In tweenhood, I inherited my aunt Zelda's old red mountain bike. She's (24)
Dad's half-sister from his father's second marriage, only five years older
than me and one of the few teenagers I knew. We didn't see Zelda often,
but she was all smile and cheer. She spoke three languages, drew fashion
illustrations, gave me her duplicate Pogs, and painted my nails with
a layer of glitter polish over contrasting opaques. I tried hands-free
riding on her bike and flipped over the handlebars. But I didn't give
up searching for my cool.

"DON'T HELP ME! Someday you won't be near to help," I screeched (25)
to a friend attempting to unsnarl me from the bike I had just crashed.
I am ten. It is summertime dusk in the middle of our suburban street.
This memory sticks like so few do. Time-stamped proof of how long
I have felt an impending and predestined aloneness. Maybe I thought
people were going to leave me, not realizing that more often it would
be me that wasn't able to stay.

(26) By teenhood, we had moved to an area of farmland being converted
      into a new suburban development. It was still disconnected from the
      rest of the city, a thiry-minute drive to the grocery store. A yellow
      minibus was sent to collect the small group of us older kids to be taken
      forty-five minutes away to the nearest school. The only other way to
      get around was to persuade a reticent parental chauffeur. It was a dirt
      sketch of a community—fields and forest plowed into muddy mounded
      lots. Geoglyphic gravel roads foreshadowed the crescents and cul-de-
      sacs to come, already named after the nature that was stripped to make
      them: Otter Tail, Mud Creek, Owls Cabin, Mountain Meadows. Just
      like the neighborhood I left, pathways had been paved around these
      invisible homes. I was becoming body-conscious. Biking became my
      primary exercise. I would ride around the paths after school for the few
      months a year that weren't wet and cold. Occasionally I would find a
      ravine with a stream or a half-built tree house and perch for a while
      in reverie. I was finally old enough to roam beyond sight of home, or
      perhaps we had just moved somewhere that had childproofed itself.
      I couldn't get lost because eventually the paths would loop back to
      familiar territory or dead-end at a country field. Even so, it was the
      first opportunity to be the decider on when to stay or leave the place I
      was left. Life was no longer a shuttle between school and home. There
      was a third option of fringed elsewhere to seek refuge.

(27) Not too far past the farmland sat Ottawa International Airport. It was
      close enough to spot planes on angled ascents from our dinner table.
      Almost as close as when a hot-air balloon is flying above and you can
      see the passengers waving from the basket—evidence that humans too
      could be skyborne things. Once the moon hung large and low, and a
      plane flew right across in perfectly framed silhouette like the scene in
      E.T. where the boy and alien cross the night sky on a bicycle. *Empire*
      magazine named that scene the most magical movie moment of all time.

I soon outgrew Zelda's bike and resorted to using Mom's blue bike. (28)
I have no memories of my mother on a bicycle or us going on a ride
together. Her bike was old but not in a cool way. It was grimy, the gears
didn't shift, and it went *clankety clank queek qing ding ding* when I
rode it. Sometimes a piece of metal or a screw would fly off. I reported
to my parents that this was a hazard to all the bystander babies and
gravel-licking toddlers that saturated our neighborhood (hinting at
my need for a new bike). They rolled their eyes. Our construction-
site-wasteland community was more hazardous than the bicycle.

When I was fourteen, I came home from school to find my parents at (29)
the top of the staircase asking me to come into their bedroom. Dad
was never home from work this early. Mom and Dad rarely operated
as a unit. My immediate guess was that they were surprising me with a
new bike. What girl, who has never been gifted a surprise, assumes that
a month before Christmas, three months before her birthday, amidst
the frigid billow of Canadian winter, she will receive a bicycle from
her parsimonious parents? Me. The perennial hoper in the footholds
of Friday's possibility. Spoiler: my sparkly magenta bike was the only
bike ever purchased for me by someone else. They had brought me
into their room to repeat the speech that they had given separately
to each of my sisters that day. We were getting divorced. Midway
through their speech I was still holding hope that the news would be
sweetened by a bike.

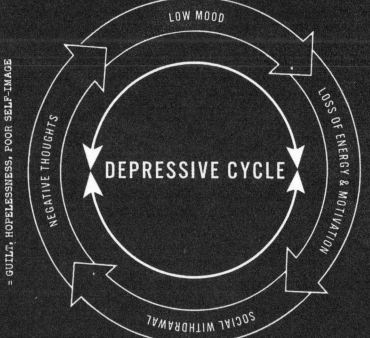

= SADNESS, DESPAIR, DARK DARK DARK

LOW MOOD

= GUILT, HOPELESSNESS, POOR SELF-IMAGE

NEGATIVE THOUGHTS

= FATIGUE, LETHARGY, LANGUIDNESS

LOSS OF ENERGY & MOTIVATION

DEPRESSIVE CYCLE

SOCIAL WITHDRAWAL

= AVOIDING SOCIAL + EXTRACURRICULAR ACTIVITIES

As a toddler, *The Wizard of Oz* played often on our television. In sepia, (30)
Dorothy sings about dreamlands beyond the rainbow that she can't
reach. It is the only song with words I learned on the piano before
quitting at age eight. I would sing along to the keys on a loop while kids
played together outside the window. I sang it with that same aching
for somewhere else. Miss Gulch rides by on her bicycle as Dorothy
finishes singing and, soon after, past Dorothy's bedroom window as
her house gets lifted up into the tornado. Miss Gulch and her bicycle
turn into the Wicked Witch on a broom and I am petrified. Petrified by
the colorlessness and the hopelessness and the storm and the cackling
witch. I never made it to Technicolor Oz. I never watched Dorothy
learn her happiness could be found at home.

From a distance my childhood home looked like any other family's. (31)
Four pretty daughters who were kempt, well-mannered, never missed
class, ate nutritious snacks, were taught to read and multiply before
primary school. A house just so with the trendiest décor. Parents that
were liberally minded, smart, and honorable. My report card was
straight As, my bed every day made. I gave the custodian and bus
driver holiday cards. Believed in forest faeries. Wished on dandelions
blown sideways. I didn't know the source of the disquietude I bore,
a dampness that muted possible highs and magnified sads. I heard
psychologist and poet Anita Barrows once call her childhood home a
"permeable darkness" for the same reason as my own. Entering my
front door was like rubber boots stepping in mud, suctioned stuck,
waters rising up, no sense trying to run from a sludge encroaching
upon whatever crepuscular rays might have crept in. It wasn't until
I faced my own bout of depression in my twenties that I understood
what Mom's mental health had meant for child-me. She set the tone for
how free our souls could be. They were clogged with her languor, to the
few rooms she hardly left long enough to watch our gaiety, let alone
provoke much more. The cycle of depression didn't just entrap her; it

cycled through each of us, our linings left moldy. I had few models for what joy and celebration could be achieved in domesticity amidst all the anxiety and ennui. I didn't observe home as a place where anyone was happy to be. It made it far too easy to leave.

(32) My body unintentionally learned orgasm while doing bicycle crunches. I was sixteen and diving deep into yoga-pilates fusion workout videos. The abs-obliques crunch loosely resembles a cyclist's form, supposing it were possible to ride a bike while lying on one's back and supposing said cyclist hadn't noticed that the bike had vanished from in between her. Enough bikeless cycles combined with other ab-targeted leg lifts and one might rouse a *coregasm*. But an orgasm doesn't remind me of biking. It feels like how an Atolla jellyfish looks propelling through the deep sea and how Paper Route's "Dance on Our Graves" sounds at four minutes fifteen seconds to around five minutes forty-three seconds.

(33) For a summer I juggled two food service jobs: one at my cousin's gour-met health restaurant, another at Domino's Pizza. I would bike to the boutique-lined Westboro Village for day shifts baking vegan desserts across the street from the Great Canadian Theatre Company, and then bike to a run-down strip mall across from the Bayshore Cineplex to join an assembly line of pizza preppers. When I biked home after closing, the air smelled like fresh-cut grass and felt like chilled glass. The ride was my buffer between worlds, a heralding to summers when time spent outside was confined only by the rising and setting sun.

(34) A coworker cautioned me about securely locking up my bike. He told me his bike was stolen the previous year. It was neon orange with a highlighter-green chain wrapped around the head tube, black electrical tape stripes on the down tube. The same day while biking home, I saw someone riding that very bike. I debated what I could do. Speed after them, accuse them of thievery, and make a citizen's arrest? Trail them

for several miles until they parked and then steal the bike back? What proof could be provided? No one prosecutes bike-snatchers.

I read an article about people who successfully retrieved their stolen (35) bikes through Craigslist, where thieves were reselling them. I read another article about a couple who would leave bikes unattended in their yard to lure thieves, and then chase them down and beat them with bats when they took the bait.

The rest of adolescence felt like spinning the wheel of a bicycle sus- (36) pended above ground. I can hear that vibrating metallic hum as the closely spaced wire spokes zip around the gear axis, visible only as dizzy glints of light fraying to blur; the wheel in constant motion, but fastened in one place.

The heart of the bike is the crankset. Its gears connect to the rear wheel (37) through a chain drive. There are two crankarms with pedals on either side of the crankset axle. The crankarms are fixed in exactly opposite positions (when one crankarm is up, the other is down). As one's feet exert force upon the pedals, the chain moves around the gears that move the rear wheel. It was once thought that to maximize efficiency, one's feet should pedal in circles with both feet maintaining consistent force at all points around the axle: as one foot pushes forward and down, the other foot should be pulling back and up on its pedal. This is referred to as "the myth of the upstroke," because research has found that our muscles are better built for the downstroke motion than the upstroke. To best exploit leg potential, a pedal stroke should start strong at the top of the circle in the *power phase*, then begin to rest as it moves down and around through the *recovery phase*. This pedaling technique is demonstrated through a "clock diagram."

The diagram of clockwise motion is true when observing the bike profile from the side with the right leg. However, if one observed

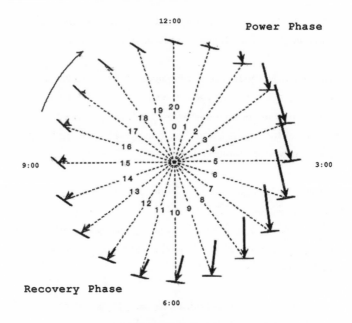

Power Phase

Recovery Phase

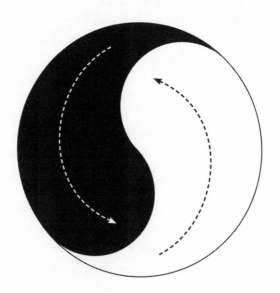

the other side of the bike as the left leg moved, the motion would appear counterclockwise. If I could observe both sides of the crankset at once, these clock arms would be moving forward and backward simultaneously—a yin-yang energy of opposing forces acting upon my revolutions.

When I graduated high school, I moved out of Mom's house into Dad's (38) apartment next to my university in downtown Ottawa. The world opened a bit in an urban setting and the proximity to activities that I could navigate on foot or public bus. Dad had a stationary exercise bike. We both used it often, he while reading, me while watching television. It had a tracker that calculated calories burned. An eternity was required to burn off a cookie (I would prefer to remain ignorant to the exercise-diet ratio). It was a slog, no changing pace with slope or enthusiasm for scenery or threat from the elements. A road to nowhere.

Coming from a large family of modest means, I was a practitioner of (39) minimalist consumption. I didn't respect material dependency or waste. I was careful with my belongings. I knew how to make things last, how to savor and be sparing, and how much of a thing could be cut away while still retaining its thingness. My first "big" purchase in adulthood was a bike: $150 from Canadian Tire, the cheapest I could find that wasn't hideous. It was a white mountain bike with purple ornamental decals that I immediately scraped off. I couldn't justify extras like a bell, so when nearing oblivious pedestrians, I would quietly squeal, "Excuse me," until eventually needing to awkwardly squeeze around them (in my next life, I will install a foghorn and sound it continually when careening through droves of pedestrians too absorbed in their selves and selfies to stay in their lane). When a bike pedal was inexplicably mangled, I replaced it with a cheap mismatched one from a used bike shop. I didn't buy lights, so I would try to return home before sunset, or sneakily take back roads and sidewalks to avoid being ticketed.

(40)   There are 680 miles of pathways in Ottawa—a labyrinthine network weaving around and through its sprawling bounds, past waterways and into forests, parks, and neighborhoods. It felt like a lifetime could be spent cycling in Ottawa without ever repeating the same route. I would regularly go explore these paths for several hours at a time in the Ottawa-Gatineau region, hardly encountering another person or car crossing. So much of the city's sublime is found only in a hidden freeze-frame tucked along these dense routes. I would turn a bend and be confronted with a wooden bridge and stream glistening through diffused rays, or a lake edged with willows, or a boardwalk under a canopy of autumnal trees scattering color. Some beauty is visible only when abutted by banality. Spots beautiful in a specific time, direction, and angle viewed from bike-height that couldn't be replicated. No matter how much I loved a new place, I rarely, if ever, returned to it. I thought there was too much else in the world to justify circling back around. I always wanted more and varied novelties to sample. The highlight reel of my plentiful and fleeting bike rides in Ottawa survive now only in sensation, not sight.

(41)   Maybe cycling is bred into Canadian citizenry. Canada has the longest recreational path in the world—the Great Trail—fifteen thousand miles meandering across to the Atlantic, Pacific, and Arctic coasts. The trail links up 80 percent of the population and 100 percent of my Canada-dwelling friends. It feels like a lighthouse that could guide me to safety if I were a fugitive, or a rare survivor of a pandemic or regional alien invasion or nuclear explosion. I could follow the trail from Ottawa to loved ones in Toronto, Thunder Bay, Calgary, Nelson, Vancouver, Victoria, or Whitehorse. A significantly lengthier commute than with a plane or a car, but in an Armageddon, I would have time, and a bike unaffected by power outages or fuel shortages to secure safe passage.

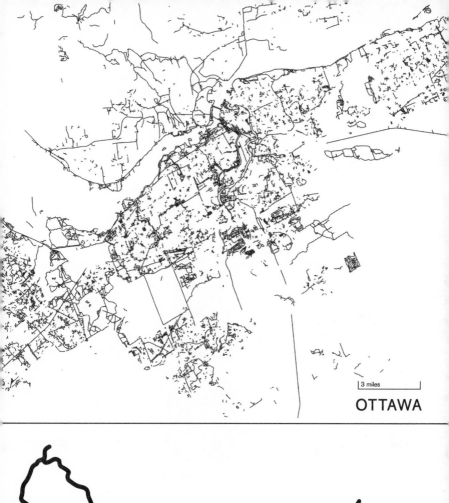

3 miles

OTTAWA

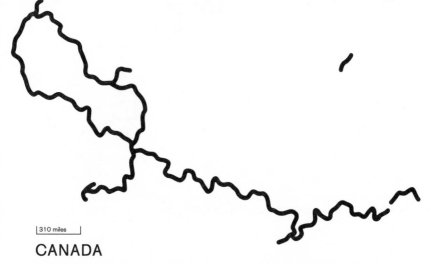

310 miles

CANADA

(42)   Historically, bicycles were the symbol of female liberation. In the late nineteenth century, women were meant to be chaperoned in public spaces and spend most of their time indoors or otherwise safely traveling by horseback or carriage. Bicycles provided freedom of movement and were at the forefront of the suffrage movement, allowing women to campaign by bicycle.

Women's rights activist Susan B. Anthony famously said, "[Bicycling] has done more to emancipate women than anything else in the world. It gives women a feeling of freedom and self-reliance. I stand and rejoice every time I see a woman ride by on a wheel . . . the picture of free, untrammeled womanhood."[3] I was continuing to become an untrammeled woman.

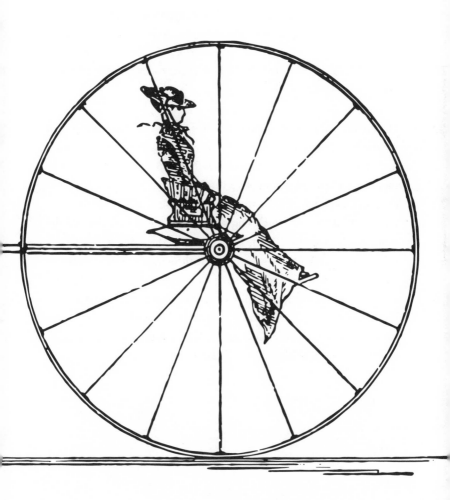

(43) In the early 1800s, inventor Karl von Drais coined the term *velo-cipede* to refer to human-powered wheeled vehicles, from the Latin for *velox*, meaning "swift," and *ped*, meaning "feet." The word *bicycle* was introduced in the 1860s, when inventors made velocipedes with pedals. However, it wasn't until the 1880s that inventors perfected a machine that resembled our modern-day conception of a "bicycle." Studying French as a child, I was taught the French translation was *la bicyclette*. But this is actually a Frenchification and, though often used interchangeably with *un vélo*, is considered by francophones as a dated term that more accurately describes bicycles that were only used by wealthy men. Ironically, in French, *bicyclette* is a feminine noun and *vélo* is masculine.

(44) I had never heard of *vélo* until I started working at a magazine shop in downtown Ottawa that claimed to have the largest selection of international newspapers and magazines in North America (this time was the cusp of the magazine industry's collapse). There were six thousand titles and no directory. I had to memorize where each title was to assist customers. It was in the cycling section that I first encountered the term: *VeloNews, Velo Vision, Top Vélo, Vélo Mag, Vélo Magazine* . . . On weekend lunch breaks, I would sift through a selection of travel magazines and scrawl on scraps the names of places I wanted to go. Did my wanderlust naturally coincide with my age, or was it intensified by the staticity of my childhood? Then, travel seemed my only avenue for escape from a preordained mundaneness. A brief adventure every so often before forcible return to sameness.

PLACES TO GO

Alaska

Yosemite

...ranger Fjord, Norway

...naktapur, Nepal

Yucatan — Guanajuato, MX

Yangon, Yangon, Myanmar

Millau Bridge, Languedoc, FR

Cape Breton, Nova Scotia, CA

Cyclades, Santorini, Greece

New York City / La Jolla, CA

Great Barrier Reef

Bogota, Colombia

Abu Simbel, Egypt

Suli, Muli Enga, Papua New Guinea

ICE CAVE — SVI...

ICELAND

Origami workshop
OBON FESTIVAL
Stained glass staircase, ...
No BORIBETSU + HORSEIDE

---

uzbery
& Tank
Market
& Mollendorf

...ty → Munich
Kleidervkrka...
...Tauber
Reichstag
→ VIEWS

GHANA

Aburi Botanical Gardens

INDIA

...aha Kumbh Mela (festival)

...rat, Gujarat (diamond polishing)

...imbay — chhaya jyotishi (measures shadow + predicts future)

Nongriat Village, East Khasi Hills District

GEORGIA

Dezertiri Market, TBILISI

ANTIGUA → island

...tba — Pink Lac
...NEGAL

...n de Broeren
...therlands

BOSNIA

...AN
Kosovo

Art + Cycling
Tour
PEPY TOURS
Cambodia

Niayesh Boutique Hotel arranges
hom...

KAZAKH...

Mashiktur

Jusup Central...

Mosque,

Pavlodar

Greenland

ITTOQQORTOORMIIT

ILLULISSAT

NUUK

TASIILAQ

...SSELFELD
...OISTERS
...VE

YEMEN —
SOCOTRA ISLAND —
trees — Wadi Ayhft

✳ Countries ✳

CUBA — Havana

TUNISIA — Medenine

KYRGYZSTAN

LEBANON — ehden
          — Tripoli
          — Beirut

KIRIBATI

NAMIBIA — Herero Tribe
          Maku...

BRAZIL

BULGARIA
→ International Festival of Masquerade Games (JAN.)
→ BABUGERI — mummers — KUKERI

...to you
Greenhouses
of
Laeken.
BELGIUM

CHINA

Dunhuang Dishu
Lijiang Impression...
Huang Long Ntl Park
Dali Village → INDIGO...
Fenghuang / Phoenix C...
Tianzi Hotel, Hebei
Xinjiang (Kashgar)
ERHAI LAKE, Yunnan

FEZ TANNERY MOROCCO

Avenue du Baobab
MADAGASCAR

WAIOTAPU THERMAL RESERVE, NZ.

Somerset Levels
Brighton
Eden Project

ENGLAND

(45)   *Velocipede* became the root word for other cycle-related terms[4]:

velocipedestrienne

a female cyclist of the 1920s

velocipathy

a belief during the Victorian era that exercise with velocipedes was valuable to the body and soul

velocipedestrianisticalistinarianologist

(one of the longest nouns) a person who studies the study of studying cycling

These words might not be in your dictionary, but that's okay, made up (46) words still matter. If I were to invent a bicycle-related word it would be *cervelo*: "bicycle brain" (root from *la cervelle*, meaning "brain" in French). When I google it, there is already a Canadian cycling manufacturer by the same name and with the same portmanteau rationale. Some might depict self-propelled gears turning in their mind, but I picture a tiny me on a bicycle powering my brain. Sometimes tiny me gets tired of pumping or spins madly.

L V P C E O E E D I. Anagrams become easier to unscramble when the (47) letters are arranged in a circle and reconfigured again, again, again, until words spring out.

```
      L                    E                      I
  E      V            E      P              L        V
D          E        D          I        O              E
I          O        E          C        P              D
  P      C            V      L            C          E
    E                    O                    E

        P  V                  D  L
    E                    I          E
    E          O        C          E
    L          I        O          E
      D  C                  V    P
        E                      E

      O                    E                      V
  L      V            D      V              E        E
I          E        E          E        D              L
C          D        I          L        E              O
  P      E            C                    P          C
    E                    P              I
```

(48)   I come across the book *Dashed against the Rock: A Romance of the Coming Age* (1894)[5]. Tantalizing. I flip the pages and land on a section with six sequential book plates of circle diagrams. The preceding text explains that a molecule has three envelopes. Of greatest interest is the rotating or etheric envelope, which, were it arrested, would release an astounding volume of matter far greater than it housed in its motion. Google's opinion of this book: no comment. I type in "etheric envelope." It's referenced in a Rudolf Steiner book, a yoga farm video, a listing for body oil, and a robust site on sympathetic vibratory physics. The site credits John Ernst Worrell Keely with developing this molecular morphology "before there was a quantum anything"[6]. I google "John Keely." Biographies describe him as a mechanical experimenter, a physician, a pharmacist, a painter, a carpenter, a carnival barker, a professor of perfidy, a scandalous scamp, a fraudulent inventor.[7] Keely swindled investors out of millions of dollars over twenty-five years as he claimed to be constructing a "Hydro-Pneumatic-Pulsating-Vacuo-Engine" that harnessed the etheric force within water molecules to create unlimited energy. The press called it a *perpetual motion machine*.

I google "perpetual motion." The term is always latched to "machine." *To move forever in a closed system without additional energy inputs.* Inventors and scientists, dating back to Indian mathematician Bhāskara II in 1150 CE, have tried to design such a machine, usually using a similar overbalanced wheel model. The Bhāskara wheel had curved spokes partly filled with mercury so, as the wheel turned, weight would be unevenly distributed around the rim to center and maintain a propulsive force. The design doesn't work. No subsequent machine has either. And inventors like Keely were actually trying to make *over-unity* machines that would not just endlessly maintain their own motion but generate excess energy for extraction. I learn perpetual motion is impossible because of physics, friction, gravity. It violates the first two laws of thermodynamics: (1) energy cannot be created or destroyed, only altered; (2) an isolated system will move toward entropy. Even celestial bodies will one day succumb to burnout.

In Keely's time, there were other perpetual motion hoaxes. The nineteenth century was a time of public curiosity for new sciences. There was/is so much not yet seen or known. Keely died before he was found out, so I won't presume he was a pseudoscientific scam artist without genuine belief in his theories. Some still believe in him, in perpetual motion, in the fragility of modern science. For the last decade, physics professor Donald Simanek has kept a long updated list on his site of answers to questions people e-mail him about perpetual motion machines.

Isn't anything possible if you are clever enough?
No . . . The geometry of our universe makes many things impossible, and physics laws are all constrained by that geometry . . . You can't design a walking path in a closed loop that is downhill all the way, in either direction. Nature has many impossibilities. The laws of physics that we have discovered tell us what nature can, and can't do.[8]

(49)   Once asked how he maintained his stamina at eighty-seven years old, Noam Chomsky responded, "The bicycle theory. As long as you keep riding, you don't fall."[9]

(50)   Since the nineteenth century, scientists have tried to explain exactly how bicycles maintain self-stability—how when a bicycle is moving forward fast enough (sans rider), it resists tipping over. In part this is due to the *gyroscopic effect*—the law of conservation of angular momentum states that a body that is rotating around its own axis has the tendency to maintain its own direction.

(51)

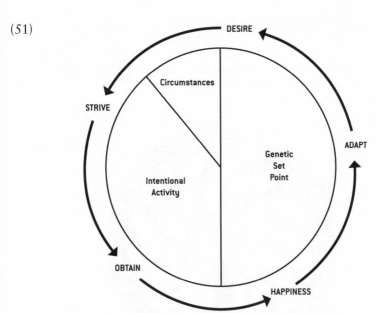

I worry about what would happen if I stopped pedaling my cervelo forward. Back in the 1970s, Philip Brickman and Donald T. Campbell coined the term *hedonic treadmill* in their essay about relative happiness.[10] They theorized that each person has a happiness set point that may fluctuate in the short term given external fortunes and failures, but eventually adapts back to a natural set point. Some call this never-ending dissatisfaction the "Cycle of Desire." It's part of what makes us human, the drive for expansion. More recent studies on DNA variants have found around 50 percent of our happiness is inherited, with the remainder governed by environment and life circumstances. I am riddled with depressed genes. Sometimes I feel like I awake at a set point of 0 percent, the entirety of my well-being conditional on my effort and capped at a peak of the 40 percent I can control. Suggestions for how to overcome the cycle of one's set point is to redirect energy from hedonic pursuits to eudaimonic goals—seeking meaning over pleasure, serving others, living virtuously.[11] This can involve disrupting repetition through new experiences or reorienting one's gaze and speed within the repetition in order to notice unexplored aspects of the common.

When I got mosquito bites as a child, I would slice stars into their (52) centers with my thumbnail, replacing the itch with a piercing pain.

I still mark my forearm this way when I start to get carsick, or my stomach flip-flops on amusement park rides, or my anxiety is running high. At my will, the little asterisks sidetrack an undesirable condition with a note reading, *Look here! Focus on this and not that!* This trick was based on a general understanding that the body processes only one painful stimulus at a time, the rest fading as the most intense signal is prioritized. I move through my goals that way too, focusing on the brightest star rather than the whole dark sky. I think if I were to stop staring at a star for too long, the galaxy would so overwhelm my senses that there would be no North Star to guide my course. Then I might tip over.

(53)   Next to Charlevoix Bridge in Montreal, there is an offshoot from the
       bike path that shimmies along the canal. Like the main bike path, it
       too is paved with a yellow line painted up its center, only rather than
       leading a cyclist across the city, it will detour them into 131 feet of
       knotted loops and sharp angles before sending them back down and
       out the same way they came. The path is the work of sculptor Michel
       de Broin, who was inspired by *gestural abstraction*—an artistic process
       that focuses on the physical action of painting instead of the visual
       outcome of the work.[12] The *how* is the point: intuitive, unplanned
       splattering, spraying, smearing, splotching, drip-dropping. De Broin
       says the freehand-drawing-turned-pathway is meant to confront the
       rationalism imposed by urban planning in public spaces. While not all
       lines of motion through a city are straight, I think the compact delir-
       ium of de Broin's intervention might hamper a cyclist long enough to
       consider the external control being imposed upon them by any path
       and what awaits them outside of these lines, or maybe the path makes
       them hyperfocused on their every move and thought, or dizzy and so
       contained that exiting back to a fluid route revitalizes gratitude.

       In French the work is entitled *Entrelacement*, which is also the term
       for a medieval literary technique that braids textual and/or pictorial
       subplots into a larger narrative.[13] Digressions and motif are designed
       to feel like a bewildering maze of disordered events from the inside,
       but once on the outside as integral multiplicity that better represents
       how people perceive the complexity of life than would a simple,
       chronological story.

(54)   Bicycle paths between and within cities are inconsistent. The safest are the strips brightly painted green indicating *bicycles belong here*, best when elevated next to sidewalks or with curb barricades on either side. The most dangerous are the occasional bicycle symbols stenciled on the tarmac that suggest *follow me* before vanishing mid-route on a shoulderless highway. There are roads with no demarcations for bikes, others with painted lines to the right of the cars, to the left of the cars, between parked cars and the sidewalk. There are also those informal shortcuts—*desire paths*—trodden through grass betraying an oversight in traffic planning. I like those most for their refusal to obey some cockeyed edict, for the will in dredging their own way. I am averse to being told where to go. I want to be like an early explorer (minus the colonization and disease), sailing around edges to shade in shapes I eponymously claim, affinities ordered by an internal compass in conference with storm gods each day.

(55)   In middle school, rubber bracelets were a very popular accessory distributed by charities to allies. This began with yellow rubber bracelets debossed with the word LIVESTRONG. At the time, what I knew was this was Lance Armstrong's charity. After he had cancer, Lance Armstrong was the only professional cyclist I could name. I knew that Armstrong won (or completed) the Tour de France many times, and maybe he was the best or the fastest or some other *–est*. And for a while, that was impressive and he was a celebrity. And then there was scandal involving drugs possibly enhancing Armstrong's performance. And now I am not sure what society's opinion is of him or who dethroned him in Tour de France fame. All I knew about the Tour de France was that it was a race on roads in France. At least I thought it was a race; *tour* more accurately translates to a circuit than a competition. I assumed it was one of the oldest or hardest or most important cycling events in the world. Witnessing history unfold as I age is a smattering of fragmented memories that get assembled into

something I come to confuse with facts. Especially when it pertains to peripheral culture. The competitive cycling world feels antithetical to my practical cycling. It is about competition and speed, and a pace and path dictated by someone else.

AN INCOMPLETE LIST OF BIKE TOPICS NOT IN THIS BOOK (56)

animals riding bicycles
(bears, monkeys, elephants,
dogs, raccoons . . .)

existence of any bike memes,
viral videos, hashtags, boycotts

the bicycle habits of billionaires,
world leaders, celebrities

spoke card history

best bike brands and companies

types of bike locks, bike racks

bike seat shapes

why bicycle streamers are no
longer in vogue . . . are they?

how often to pump your tires

bike repair know-how

where bikes go to die,
what bike parts are recyclable,
bike graveyards

Ai Weiwei installations

if bicycles abandoned on street
poles ever get removed, who
removes them

whether the red taillight should
flash or be constant

bicycle laws here and elsewhere

bicycle patrol

tips and tricks for cycling
in rain or snow

statistical probability of getting
in a bike vs. car accident

ranking of places where bikes
are least popular and why

carfree cities

Ciclovía

bicycle use by demographic

adaptive bicycles for riders
with disabilities

how long a pregnant person
can comfortably ride a bike

the difference between mountain
bike racing and trials

the difference between track
cycling and cyclo-cross

domestiques

cycling legends

cycling BMX freestyle at
the Olympics

bike surfing, artistic cycling

cycling through water in Bokrijk

zip line cycling

bicycle musems

Bicycle® Playing Cards

"Bicycle Repair Man,"
Monty Python's Flying Circus

David Byrne

(57) The same bike races are held each year, but unlike annual marathons, the bike courses never follow the same route. Sample routes for some of the world's more infamous cycle events:

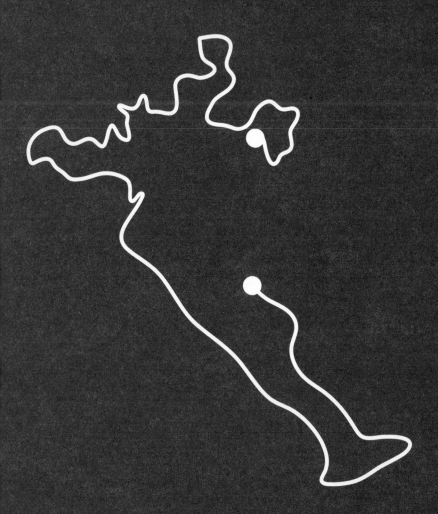

GIRO D'ITALIA
ITALY — 24 days — 2,172 miles

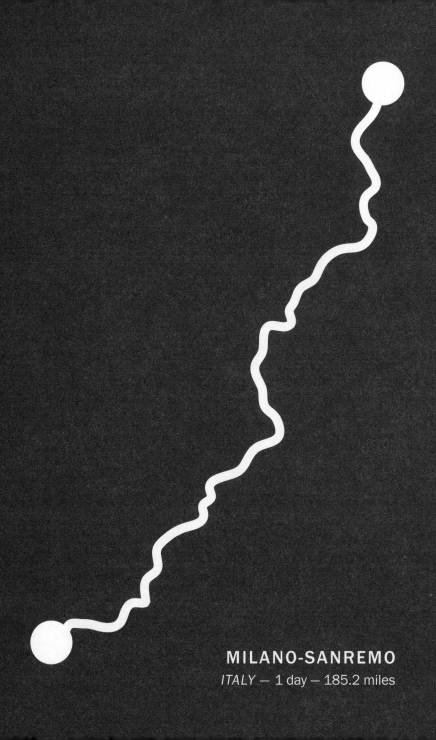

MILANO-SANREMO
ITALY — 1 day — 185.2 miles

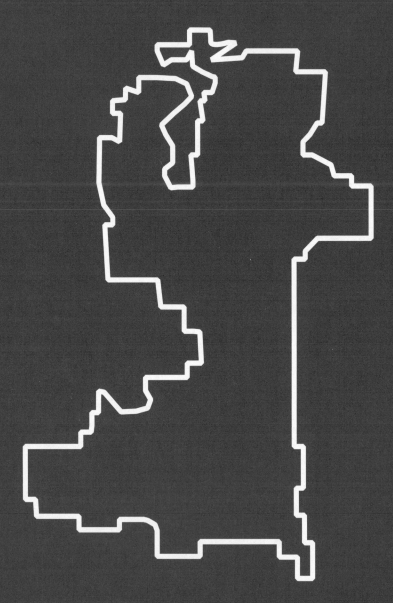

DIRTY KANZA
USA — 1 day — 200 miles

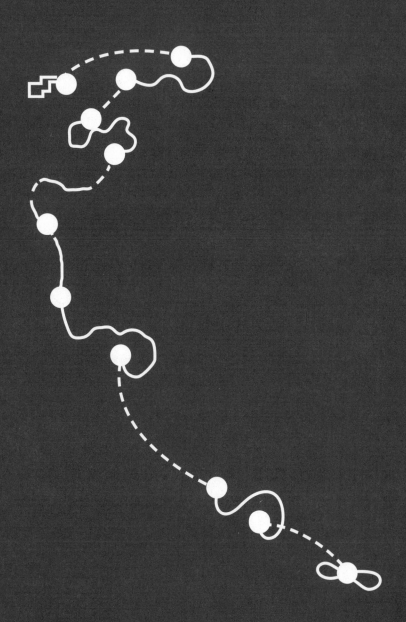

AMGEN TOUR OF CALIFORNIA

USA — 8 days — 650–700 miles

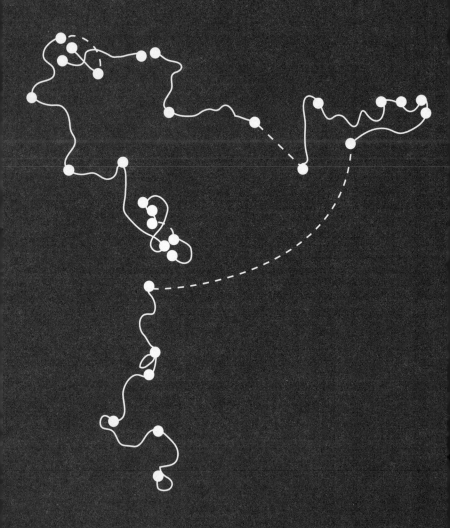

VUELTA A ESPAÑA

SPAIN — 23 days — 2,119 miles

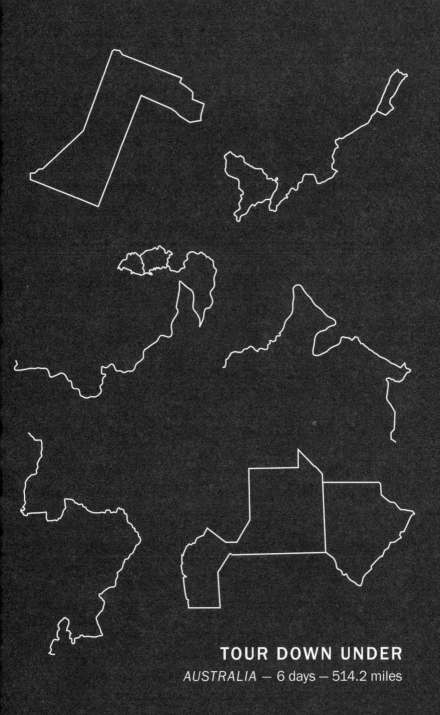

TOUR DOWN UNDER

AUSTRALIA — 6 days — 514.2 miles

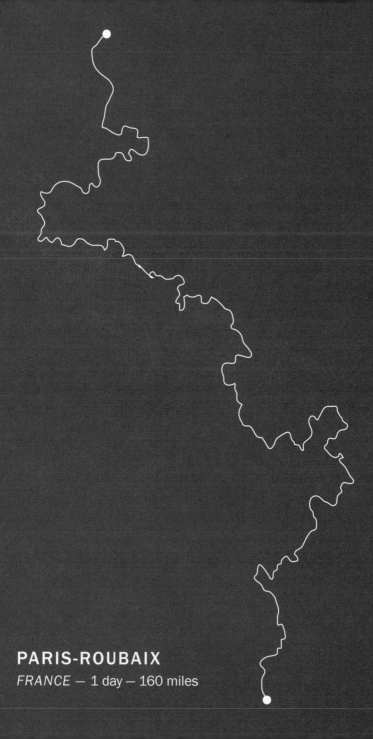

PARIS-ROUBAIX

FRANCE — 1 day — 160 miles

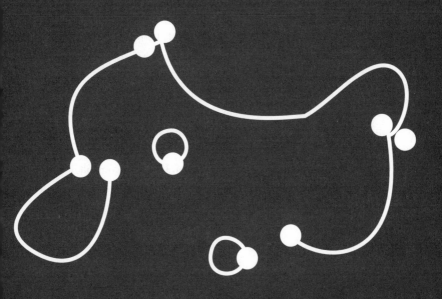

TOUR DE SUISSE
SWITZERLAND — 9 days — 728.7 miles

(58) At a party, a woman was telling me about how her friend's boyfriend had been hit and killed while riding his bicycle a month earlier. Mid-story, she received a phone call that that same friend had just been hospitalized for being hit by a car while cycling.

(59) The frequency with which bicyclists are hit on the road makes me believe it is a rite of passage and that not having personally been hit is an indicator that I have yet to achieve true bicycler status. This inference might stem from humanity's positive spin on suffering: battle scars earn us glory.

(60) The closest encounter I've had with roadside peril was in a sleepy residential Santa Cruz neighborhood. I was cycling a path running parallel to train tracks. I followed the stops and goes of the intersection markers. A car bolted down the street over the slime-green bike crossing as I rolled onto it. I slammed on the brakes and was yanked forward and under the bumper of the car as it halted inches from my skin. As I dragged the bike and myself onto the sidewalk, the car sped off. People stopped to check on me and curse the car. I cried uncontrollably and bled some. There were no grand lessons learned to better prepare for next time. The sum of my life didn't refract off the precipice of death. Everything could have changed right then, and I would have had no say in it. But nearly nothing changed then, and the difference between the two scenarios and the hundred in between would have had the same crescendo. It wasn't a story to thematically nestle here. I fell off a bike into a car, and now my body feels like it fell off a bike into a car.

(61) On the job site Monster.com, an article compiles a list of weird interview questions that recruiters suggest candidates be prepared to answer. "If you were a part on a bicycle, what would it be and why?" I am the type of person that asks questions like this in conversation. I ask, not with the intention to engineer a personality profile based on

a given response, but to transcend small talk. Random hypothetical questions make my mind feel like it's scurrying up a sand dune. The scramble energizes. I ask questions that I myself am not yet prepared to answer, but I will try, even if no one asks. What of the response are job interviewers analyzing? Are they watching for one's good humor in indulging the question? One's verbal thought process in arriving at a response? Do they possess a rubric that equates each part to traits suitable for a certain position? A self-identified "cyclist enthusiast" on Quora.com puts forth such a rubric.[14]

BIKE PART	TRAIT
BRAKES	You can depend on
WHEELS	Keep you going IF you need them
FRAME	Eccentric personality
FORK	Does all the work
HANDLEBARS	Very nice to touch, pretty person, reliable!
CHAIN	Manager of rear and front chainrings
REAR DERAILLEUR	Someone taking orders and doing their job
CRANKS	A good colleague, best friend, you go together
SADDLE	Someone who is being sat on a lot
FRONT DERAILLEUR	Old-fashioned worker soon forced to retire

What does it say about me that I don't want to be one part but the entire bike? Maybe that I am an artist and shouldn't be hired for the job of teammate.

(62) Answers to the *Family Feud* question "Tell Me a Part of a Bicycle That Would Be Tough to Ride Without":

PEDALS	25	CHAIN	12
SEAT	23	BELL	3
WHEELS	21	BRAKES	3
HANDLEBARS	12		

(63) One of my student jobs was at Global Affairs in the government. I was responsible for daily reporting of relevant articles from international media outlets. My boss was an eccentric melophile nearing retirement. Every time he called me over to chat, I would return to my desk with a pile of CDs to listen through. The song typifying that summer was Katie Melua's "Nine Million Bicycles." It was an odd juxtaposition, entering a windowless gray cubicle each day to vagabond to distant lands via a computer screen. Soundtracking my whipped scan of global news stories, the lyrics about the universe's edge being *twelve billion light years* away, in a world of *six billion people* and *nine million bicycles* in Beijing, cast me in a hazy sway where I envisioned the world as a slow-motion blur of crowds riding bicycles in perpetuum toward an edge never to be reached. Was I experiencing the blight of fluorescent lighting or the catalyst for a beyond becoming?

(64) After founding the People's Republic of China in 1949, the Chinese Communist Party centered bicycles in its ambitious plans to improve transportation. China became known internationally as the Kingdom of Bicycles, with a mandated production of twenty-five million bicycles

中国 上海
SHANGHAI CHINA
飛輪牌
氧化鋁砂布
FLYINC WHEEL
ALUMINIUM OXIDE CLOTH
Superior Quality
NO.2½

a year. The Party empowered a factory in Tianjin to become the leading manufacturer with its "Flying Pigeon" bicycle. By the 1970s, the
factory was making ten thousand bicycles a day as post-Mao leader
Deng Xiaoping dreamed of a "Pigeon in every household." There were
long waiting lists to own one, built to last lifetimes.[15] Today over half
a billion Flying Pigeons fill the streets of China. There is a traditional
Chinese idiom that still circulates, *san zhuan yi xiang* ("three rounds
and one sound"), which refers to the four necessities of life affluent
men traditionally aspired to provide a bride to begin their home: (a
round face of) a watch, (a round spindle of) a sewing machine, (a round
wheel of) a bicycle, and a radio.[16] I wish my needs could stop at four,
though I'm confident that if they did, a bicycle would make the cut.

(65)   After government workdays, I would meet up with my friend Elizabeth
and we would go on bike rides. Elizabeth had a vintage magenta bicycle
with a wire basket on the back. The basket was always being used in
pretty ways to transport baguettes, bouquets, and sidewalk finds to
her little rental house. She had found the bike in the basement of a
Toronto thrift store just as indie-pop singer Feist was eyeing it. After
some repartee, Elizabeth won out, and a decade later, the bike is now
stationed in the house Elizabeth owns in Whitehorse, Yukon. Elizabeth
carried that bike with her to every city she lived, in the same way that
we carried each other through every milestone of our twenties. We
didn't leave the important stuff behind.

(66)   Christmas 2010, Elizabeth and I went to India. New to the heritage
and ways of an Asian city, everything appeared locomotive, chroma,
ravenous, and willful. Before sunrise on a morning in Old Delhi, we
joined a bike tour led by a Dutchman. The streets were thick with
commerce and commute. Bicycles, motorbikes, animal-pulled carts,
cows, camels, stray pets, rickshaws, trucks, all sorts of contraptions
pulling heavy loads; rows of crouched workers eating on the curb or

bathing with buckets; stalls toppled with inventory. Overhead hung heavy with electrical wires. In the spice market, women sold flowers, wove them into garlands, scattered them in our bike baskets. Sacks were being delivered, shop gates were opening, babies were tucked into the ruckus, any ground left between transport was littered with rubbish, muddy potholes, and teeming with pedestrians and children, in uniforms to rags. My slow racing days proved useful. We had to maneuver with deftness and balance, ready to seize an opening to progress onward. We turned corners I didn't think were there. It was frightening at first, dozens of close calls, but I soon grew accustomed to the disorder, reacting to what was in front of me, not behind. On the bike I felt instantly embraced by people; I would lock eyes with others and smirk in mutual recognition of the hysteria as they accepted me into the action, adjusting their patterns based on my movements as if we were one organism. I was both blissfully intoxicated and stung awake, every muscle activated, mind surging with new inspiration and perspectives beyond what I ever before had seen or imagined, too fast to absorb the majesty of the surrealist scape that surrounded.

The bicycle's business in daily life is vast. I've seen enough children (67) to fill a minivan wedged in front and behind pedalers on single bikes. Sometimes a chair without legs, a laundry basket, or a crate of some sort would be strapped over a back wheel to cradle a baby or chickens. There were bundled materials like haystacks, metal pipes, or recyclable waste reaching wide or high more than moose-sized. The add-ons seemed to have no circumscription, as long as they were securely fastened and kept steady by the owner, who may still have had an exposed seat to ride or might have needed to walk beside their versatile cargo carrier.

(68) An organization called the Otesha Project gave a presentation at my university about the bicycle tours it ran across Canada. I was intimidated by bikepacking. I didn't think I could acquire all the right gear, build up the necessary endurance, and sacrifice so much unpaid time to it. I wish I had been braver and not so hasty and frugal. I wish I had believed that I could have been as much a long-distance cyclist as any other twenty-something. But I believed in my readiness for other treks. The presenters said *otesha* was Swahili for "reason to dream" or "cause to grow." That's what I was beginning to find in adulthood. My approach to student life was becoming one of economizing non-classroom time. I had a day planner divided into thirty-minute slots, all of which would be assigned to social engagements, part-time jobs, school, exercise, and volunteering. Reading weeks, exam periods, holiday interludes, and any classroom-based courses that could be swapped for alternative forms of credit would be seized for travel, exchanges, internships, and independent study in foreign settings. The gift of living rent-free at Dad's meant that all my work placements, multiple part-time jobs, and scholarship earnings could be saved and spent on such opportunities. My growing freedom was being purchased, not just with the privilege of a supportive family, but the privilege of a supportive country and institutions that met my tenacity with resources.

(69) I was selected for a field research course in Nairobi. Our intrepid cohort was led through organized study and adventure. I would come to emulate the confidence of those I met abroad who voyaged to the world's farthest nooks. I became instant friends with a classmate, Sailor, on this course, both of us starting to ask life to keep up with our traveling spirits. Dad joined Sailor and me for a week in the Maasai Mara. We stopped in Hell's Gate National Park, rented bikes, and spent the day stalking zebras. Dad and I were both avid amateur photographers, but Dad was desperate to photograph them close-up. The zebras were savvy responders to perceived threats (at least in the shape of

a middle-aged man in tear-away cargo pants and fitover sunglasses). I watched in amusement as they would nonchalantly shuffle farther afield each time Dad cycled in their direction, abandoned his bike, and skittered into savanna. He tried standing long and still, thinking they would eventually grow comfortable and distracted and he could skulk closer. They were too smart for that. I was smart too. I would bike ahead so when he scared them away, the zebras would flee in my direction for their class portrait.

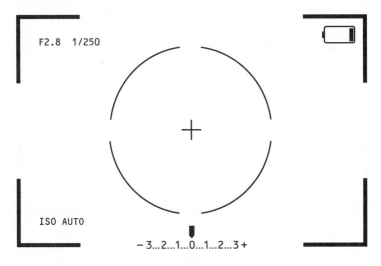

Later that night on our ride back to camp, Sailor asked, "Have you ever considered just putting the camera down and being fully present in the moment?" No. What I had thought was that if I ever lost my camera, the moment would be lost too, and I might as well not have experienced it at all. Just as I refuse to read a book without a pencil in hand. Observation feels too passive without a receptacle, almost a partial experience that is incomplete until I transform it into something new. I remember only that which has been customized through my retellings in journals, boxed artifacts, art projects, and photographs, or twice baked by an activity that is both physically active and socially connective. Travel photography was a digestible means of taking in the outrageous sensations of the unfamiliar, like freeze-frames of a video reel that could be timed with my breaths, breaths hypoventilated in a paper bag, a hole expanding and contracting, the camera's aperture deciding how much light to let in, a lens allowing focus to zoom in or out. Sailor was right, I wasn't yet devouring a panorama, I was sipping.

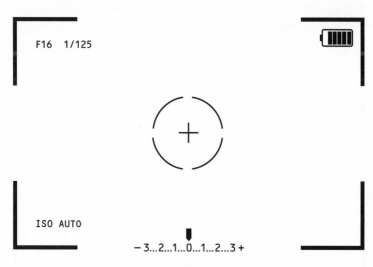

(70) Later volunteering at a tree nursery in a Kenyan village, I found myself reading a British romance novel left behind by another foreigner. Romance is not my genre, but the praise on the cover sold it as a beach read for people who hate beach reads. I think I liked it, except the protagonist dies at the end, just as she gets the love she pined for the entire novel. She is hit by a truck while idyllically riding her bike. Similar to the way that some people are convinced they will die young, it made me wonder if that's how I will end—as soon as lifelong love arrives.

(71) After backpacking down from Kenya across northern Tanzania, I stayed alone in Stone Town, Zanzibar. One day I set out for the south-

east coast to the village of Jambiani. I climbed into an empty *dala dala* for what should have been an hour's drive that took three because of all the stops made at inland market areas to pick up locals and load the minibus's roof with their bundles. I was squeezed in the dark back corner as more people continually piled in. There was a little girl in a black hijab way at the front who spent the entire journey staring at me, eyes like full moons, garbling slowly on a loop, as if hypnotized by phosphorescence "*Mzungu* . . . *mzungu* . . . *mzungu* . . . *mzungu* . . . *mzungu*" ("aimless wanderer" = foreigner = white person). How strange to be an exotic thing after a lifetime of plebeianism. I was shepherded out of the minibus when passing Jambiani. It was low season, so the skeletal town was hollowed out of any tourist goods or folks. In moments, the Indian Ocean was stretched out before me. I knelt down into the whitest sand on the emptiest beach, gobsmacked by the turquoise water. That color doesn't exist in nature. And on such a scale. I had to transmute to contain its latitude. I was capsized by the blinding blue that made me feel like a watercolor liquefying across a blank page. Like I was infinite and of nothing in Elysian Plains.

A boy of my age named Andwele approached. As a female solo traveler, this is how it went. Men would follow me attempting conversation, which at times I would aggressively try to dismiss, leading to further harassment. More often, I would smile and try to politely appease, which would only spur their stay. Andwele was nice, and while I would have preferred to be left alone, the company was easier than risking an upset. We rented bikes and rode for several hours, passing through village lives being led, nearside the coast on a gravel path with many large stones jutting out that made the trip arduous, my body painfully jostled and dehydrated in the afternoon sun, my time held hostage, but at least spent on a bike. Finally back in Jambiani, we dove into the blue, quenched. But floating near a stranger rather than a friend felt like a small red pustule on my sclera slightly intruding upon my view of paradise.

(72)

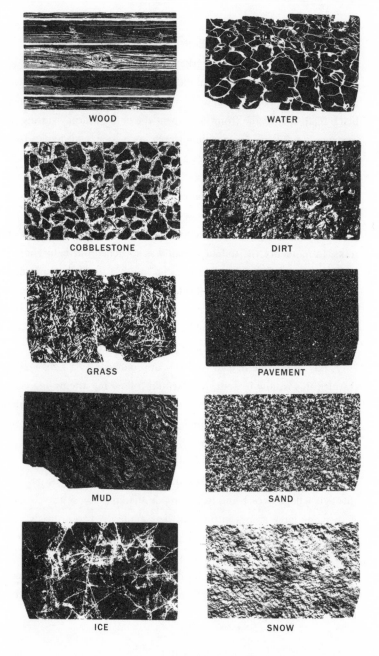

WOOD

WATER

COBBLESTONE

DIRT

GRASS

PAVEMENT

MUD

SAND

ICE

SNOW

RIDING SURFACE QUALITY

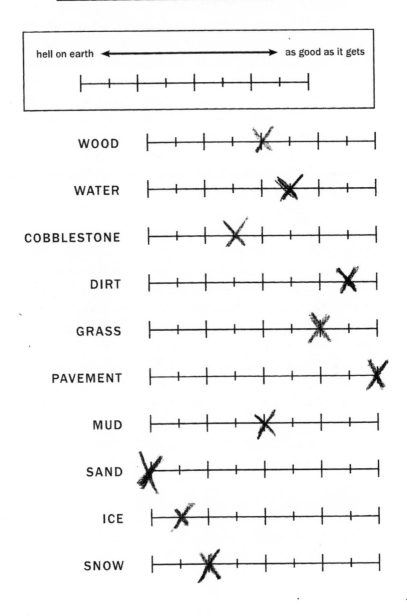

hell on earth ◄———————► as good as it gets

WOOD

WATER

COBBLESTONE

DIRT

GRASS

PAVEMENT

MUD

SAND

ICE

SNOW

(73)   The second bike I ever purchased was in Chicoutimi, Quebec, where
I did an immersive French study program. Soon after arriving I went
in search of a bike to be able to traverse the Saguenay–Lac-Saint-Jean
region. The walk to the town's thrift store felt like a concrete gutter: one
straight busy road flanked by malls and box stores in beigy-gray, void
of shade and verdancy. The store had a single bike, almost snatched
up by onlookers, in exactly my size. $65. I never walked that town's
sprawl again. The only walking was done on a single slope leading
down from the university to the river. Chicoutimi is home to one of
the steepest streets in the world, and much of the downtown area
was at such a vertical slant that biking up would be impossible and
biking down would be a death sentence. Others might have loved that
easy-access roller coaster, but plummeting out of control is not a rush
I seek. I cycled every day along rivers, breaking at different parks for a
swing. I was in the midst of a severely depressive state, and the cycling
and swinging were the only things that calmed me. There was a boy
with a bike whom I liked. Sometimes we would meet at the boardwalk and bike to get ice cream and French fries (or would they just be
called fries?). At the end of a ride, I told him that I liked him, which
was difficult for two reasons. One, in French the same verb is used to
say "I like you" and "I love you." Two, while I attempted to explain in
my intermediate-level French that I liked him without saying *je t'aime*,
he spoke beginner-level French and didn't understand. Or maybe he
just feigned confusion, because when I eventually caved and said it in
English, he was equally nonresponsive. This was only a micro-taste
of a term I would become well acquainted with: *la douleur exquise*.

That same summer, I volunteered on a tofu farm in Grand-Pré, Nova (74) Scotia. I was disturbed that I didn't know how most things in my life began and the steps they took to reach me. When I want to slow down and watch things grow, I go to farms. And also, like most of the places I visit, I go to audition different locations and ways of living. I would help with farmwork in the mornings. The rest of the time was mine to do with what I pleased. The farm had bikes and there were many dirt paths crisscrossing through fields linking town to coast. It was on these paths that I finally rode hands-free. My legs were strong, the land forgiving, and my balance kept. I felt as thrilled as child-me would have been. I was centered in myself, not just on the bike, but in my life as a twenty-one-year-old.

Afternoon rides would culminate at the beach. Evangeline Beach sits on the Minas Basin, which is known for some of the highest tides in the world. In the distance, the red cliffside of Cape Blomidon opens into the Bay of Fundy. Each summer, hundreds of thousands of sandpipers stop over on this beach as part of their annual migration down south. They rest and feed in the mudflats for several weeks. At low tide, the birds are so multitudinous and compactly nestled that one might mistake them for a field of rocks. At high tide, they fly together in what is called a *murmuration*—this patterned flocking that looks like wind if wind was not colored clear. It is one of the most miraculous sights I have ever seen. The photo I took of that murmuration has been my desktop background photo ever since. Every time I look at those blurred birds, my gut flutters and breath gasps, like I am swooping and painting the wind with them. I think of the birds and the bicycle and the way I was then, still sometimes am. Moments add up all the time. And you never really know when a little one will turn out to be a big one. Like how I shared a room in the farmhouse with a graphic design student who planted a seed in me about what to want next.

(75) I never know if the expression *it's all downhill from here* should be
      comforting or unsettling. Riding downhill can be a serene exhilaration
      after a strenuous climb. But it can also represent the decline after a
      peak experience. I don't want there to be an ultimate summit. Instead,
      waves. Crests falling into vales with a momentum to carry me down
      and on back up ad infinitum.

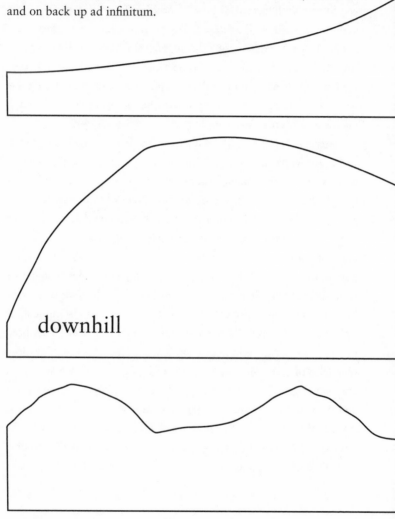

downhill

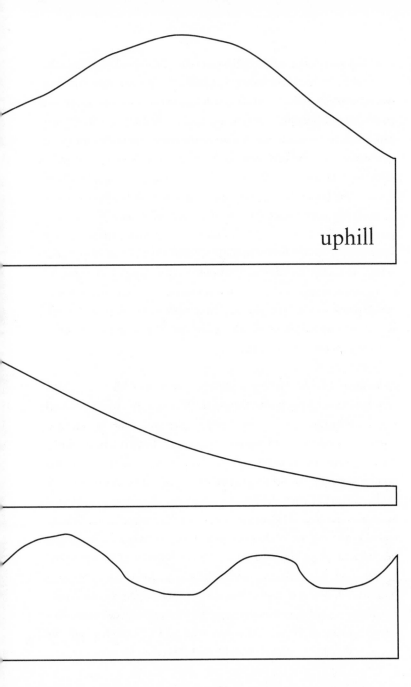

uphill

(76) Exactly a year after the Old Delhi bike tour, I attempted to conjure the magic again in Bangkok on another half-day bike tour. The tour was the same length and time of day, with just as many distinct stops—to golden-tipped Buddhist temples, a school in the Khlong Toei slum, a pad Thai café, a tiny t-shirt factory, a muay Thai gym. We traversed side streets with the odd motorcyclist passing, wide boulevards with speeding cars, and narrow canals in stilled mangrove jungle. I kept waiting for the same magic that had osmosed in India, but the more I travel, the more I discover that wonder doesn't manifest the same way twice. On the one hand, this idea can make me panic because I am a wonder addict. I want to bottle up that wonder and keep it near enough to stay hydrated. Wonder drought might be my greatest fear, to venture to a reliable well only to find it's run dry and not know what of myself or the world to believe in. On the other hand, the more I travel, the more I suspect wonder is bottomless, only the circumstances of its procurement remain a mystery.

(77) In Vietnam, I could not snap a photo of the street without a passing bicycle skimming the frame. During the Vietnam War, Viet Cong and the North Vietnamese Army outfitted bicycles with wider handlebars, reinforced suspension, and cargo pallets for civilian porters providing logistical support. These "steel horses" could haul four to six hundred pounds of supplies stealthily and freely over great distances, over jungle trails, swaying bridges, slender dikes and roads. Bicycles were credited as an essential arsenal in Vietnam's wartime endurance.[17] Load-bearing bicycles (and the now dominant motorbikes) remain an integral and flexible technology in everyday life. Vietnam is S-shaped. As we snaked up it through flattest flat rice fields, it felt like we were on the only road that existed, one vein that connected every place and this one route would take us there, eventually to all the wheres. We rode many bikes between towns and caves and water views, and while on the map our progress remained a fleck, I would have believed we had drawn that S

with inked wheels. Then, I still thought it was possible to see the whole damn world up close. I thought it possible and preferable.

I began four months of study in Bangladesh. Cycle rickshaws every-   (78)
where. I have ridden in them elsewhere—as a child in the display at the Canadian Museum of Civilization, through a Beijing hutong, to a Jaipur market, between *casa particulares* in Havana, up to Kathmandu's Monkey Temple—but never had I seen them as densely as throughout Bangladesh's cities. They are the primary mode of transport. *Guinness World Records* (2015) notes the capital Dhaka as having the most cycle rickshaws of any city in the world (there's an estimated one million rickshaws for a population of 8.9 million). They are compact enough to weave through heavy traffic, fuss-free to use in flooded streets during monsoon season, and affordably acquired and maintained by drivers who are typically of the poorest class. Bengali rickshaws are also exquisite works of art featuring people, animals, and landscapes or ornamental patterns painted and embroidered on their hoods and backsides in vibrant pigments and metallic accents.

In the first week, we studied Bangla and learned to negotiate for a fair price on our rickshaw ride from home to the university. After a few times of watching our underweight rickshaw drivers in their tartan lungis and undershirts toiling to pull us at an impressive speed in sweltering heat, we eventually reverted to walking to class along the road's uninviting edge. I am so much more a doer than a watcher, and much of what I elected to do during these trips, even when it pertained to the development projects with which I was involved, was motivated by love and curiosity. This indulgence stood in stark contrast to the realities I entered. I might say I ride to live (in a mystical sense), but a rickshaw driver rides to survive.

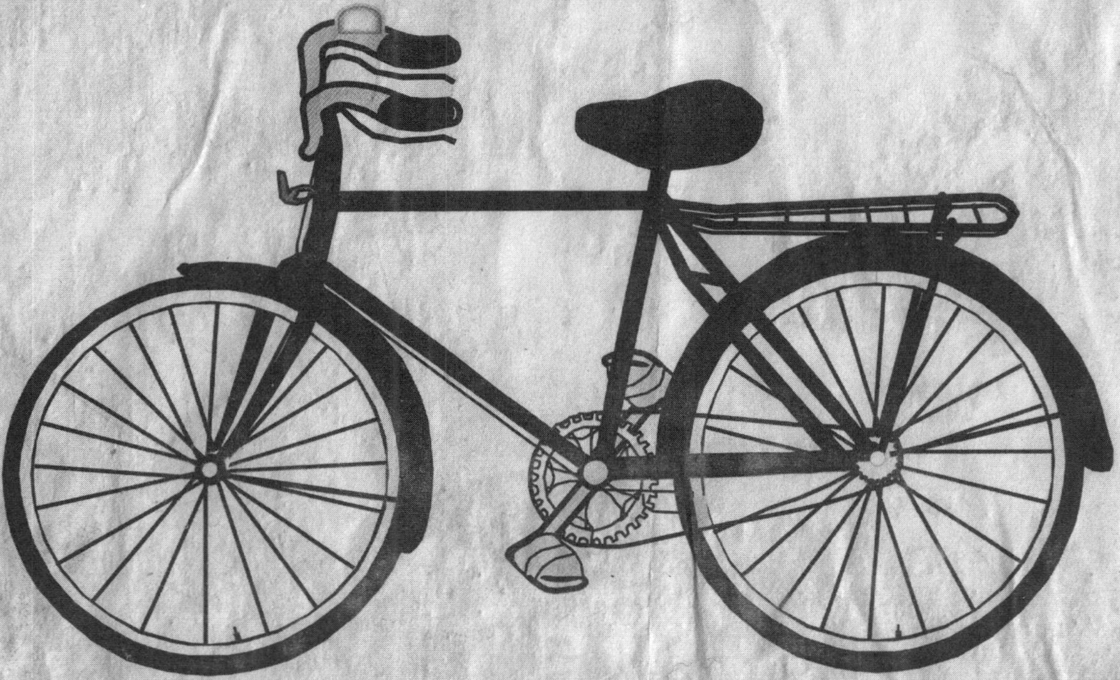

মুদ্রণে এ.এম অফসেট প্রেস, জি.এল.রায় রোড, রংপুর। মোবাইল : ০১৯৪৫৬৫৭৫৮৪

At the tea estates of Sreemangal, I went riding through the region for (79) a couple of days on a very broken undersized bike. I stopped to visit tribal minorities whose communities were tucked in the lush green hills. Steps were carved into the side of the steep hills to climb up into quiet clusters of clay homes. As a white woman, I was invited into countless homes across the country. I would sit in the middle of domestic activity, watched by the elderly, a plaything to the children, fed by a matriarch, as we all tried connecting through a combination of pidgin, gesture, and a show-and-tell of objects and images on hand. Once these tricks were exhausted, I would graciously depart and glimpse from a distance the space where I sat return to its natural order as if my existence were a figment blinked gone. Each time, I was reminded that while I was testing my aptitude for adulthood, stretching the boundaries of how far I could go into unmarked territories while still remaining intact, I was but a sideshow in other people's everyday lives.

(80) I rode one bicycle while interning in Ethiopia for a semester. I have
no proof of this. My travel journal is thin and makes no mention of
it. There is one photo that I am certain was taken on this ride, time-
stamped November 11, 2012, at 15:39 of a grandmother holding an
infant holding a spatula. My landlord had arranged for a local teen
guide to cycle with me around Lake Tana and the Blue Nile. I remember a tunnel of trees leading to Emperor Haile Selassie's palace where
the guide stopped to inform me that here is where it all began. I had
heard this many times, that Ethiopia is the birthplace of humanity and
Christianity (this is not entirely true, but also not false). But he meant
that this is where the Nile began. I had stupidly assumed, like the world
map running north to south, that Lake Tana would have been fed by
the Egyptian Nile and not the other way around. It made everything
feel upside down. No photos could be taken after this realization.

Maps inherently skew toward cartographers, what they know of
the world, what they deem important. This puny outline of reality is
amplified by GPS technology, which centers the map on the individual's
origin to destination, eliminating chance wandering, loss of time or
self. It seems this is modern society's ethos: egocentricity and efficiency
in all matters from the professional to the metaphysical. I am cultur-
ally predisposed to orientate. But I deviate. I prefer medieval mappae
mundi that fill their unknown spaces with the wondrous, outlandish,
and imaginary. I am a pilgrim not yet settled on her sacred place(s).

(81) GPS artists plot a course on a map that when cycled becomes a large-
      scale Etch A Sketch–like drawing recorded by their phone app. They
      are forcing a detour from common routes into premeditatedly random
      terrains.

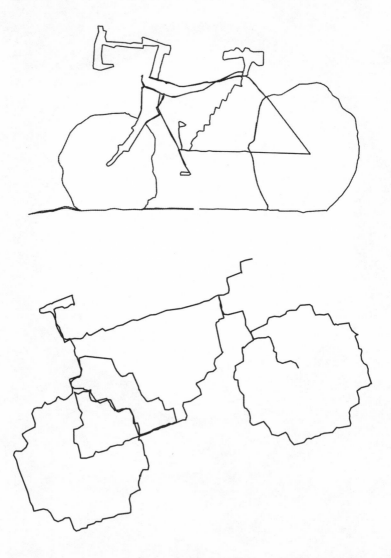

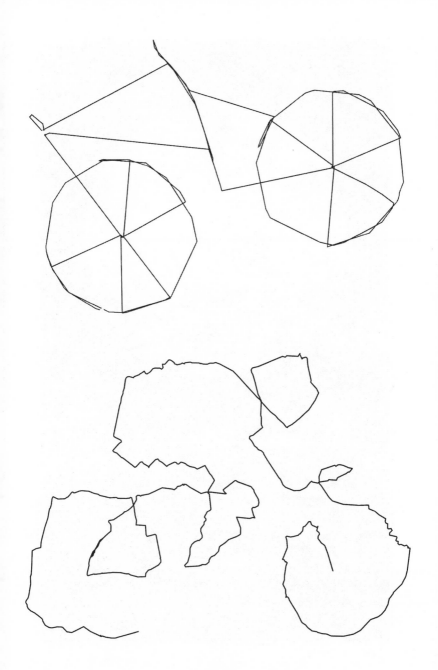

CORIOLIS EFFECT

FIGURE 1. INERTIA CIRCLES — AIR MASS IN MOTION WILL TURN
FULL CIRCLE WHEN NO OTHER FORCES ARE PRESENT

The Coriolis Effect demonstrates the pattern taken by ungrounded objects (planes, air currents, pilgrims) as they travel long distances around Earth. Objects attempting to move in a straight line will appear to deflect along a curve that is determined given the velocity of Earth in relation to the velocity of the object. Because of Earth's tilt, objects will tend to spin counterclockwise in the northern hemisphere and clockwise in the southern hemisphere, as is seen with cyclones. The effect is most prominent at high speeds or long distances. Speeds vary in different places

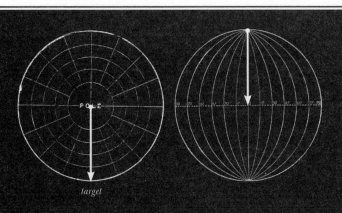

FIGURE 2. NON-ROTATING EARTH

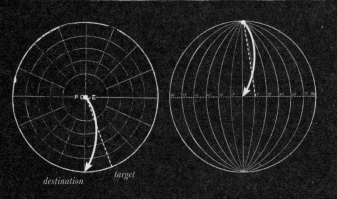

FIGURE 3. EARTH ROTATING 15° CLOCKWISE HOURLY

on Earth. An object traveling north-south will be unsuccessful at reaching its target should it attempt a straight line. From the ground, observers should factor in this effect when calculating the trajectory of an object. Objects traveling great distances and times should abandon hopes of a linear journey.

(83) After my development degree, I decided to change course and study graphic design. Had it not been for the cost of tuition, Rhode Island School of Design (RISD) would have been top of my list. All applicants to RISD are required to complete the infamous "bike home test" wherein one must draw a bicycle. The internet is littered with tortured discussion forums debating the best interpretation of this assignment. Are they evaluating creative cheekiness? Distinctive style? Or is it about accurate reproduction, maybe even done at actual size? Approaching it now, I would have made a cutout diagram that could cast a life-sized bike shadow in one's space.

(84) When I told Mom about my intentions to reroute into a creative field, she broke into a glowy proudful smile: "you have an artist's soul." I love how Mom always sanctions my every move through traits she detected in me as a tween, a toddler, a baby walking at nine months. I agree there is something about my insistence to make that seems to come by marrow. But it's a reinforcing loop: to make, I must notice, the more I notice, the more I need to make, the better I become at noticing, at making. It is often said that drawing is the skill of seeing. A renowned method, from *Drawing on the Right Side of the Brain*, for developing the basic component skills of drawing is:

1. Seeing and drawing edges and lines.
2. Seeing and drawing negative spaces.
3. Seeing and drawing relationships.
4. Seeing and drawing light and shadow.
5. Seeing and drawing the whole (*gestalt*, the essential nature of a thing).[18]

The seeing and the drawing might be my life's bones.

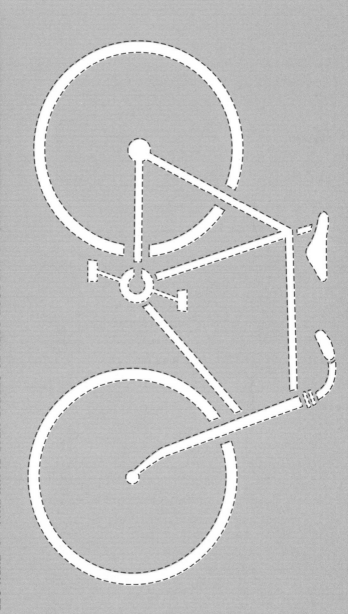

1. CUT CAREFULLY ALONG DOTTED LINES. 2. LAY BOOK OPEN TO SPREAD NEAR BLANK WALL. 3. TURN OFF LIGHTS. 4. LIFT CUT PAGE PERPENDICULAR TO SPREAD. 5. SHINE FLASHLIGHT THROUGH PAGE AND PROJECT BIKE ONTO WALL, MOVING CLOSER OR FARTHER FROM THE WALL TO CAST BIKE SHADOW TO DESIRED SIZE.

PAGE LEFT
INTENTIONALLY
BLANK FOR
BIKE CUTOUT

Try to draw a bicycle without looking at a reference. The frame cannot (85) be intuited. Amputated parts link up like an unnumbered connect-the-dots puzzle.

(86)   Some people circumnavigate the globe by bicycle, all eighteen thousand miles of land quilted together with flights over oceans. Scottish cyclist Mark Beaumont is the fastest to complete this journey at 78 days, 14 hours, and 43 minutes. He said the first time he did the trip in his twenties he was "wide-eyed and naive. There's something special about the first time you travel alone by bicycle," but a decade later when he did the trip again, older and faster, "it made the world feel absolutely, gigantically tiny."[19] I think I hold both feelings at once.

(87)   I often find myself inhabiting a state of dualism. One dialectical duality that surfaces is between what of me is from Mom versus Dad. Mom is bound to home; everything that matters and is manageable is inside. If I want to see her, I must go visit her micro-world. For Mom, life is too long; for Dad, life is too short. He wants to live forever so he'll have time to see and learn everything. I mostly see Dad *out there* as our travels intersect. I am held by this dueling desire to turn inward and outward, to stay and go, to look toward a home and a road.

(88)   For a few months I moved into Dad's new home with his new wife while I took another student job in government downtown. The bike ride to work was seventy-five minutes along the Ottawa River, through shady forests and greenspace, past the gates of Parliament and the Gothic Revival buildings of sandstone with copper green roofs. It was faster than the three buses that could get me there, but swelteringly muggy. Summers in Ottawa averaged 95°F with the humidex. By the time I reached work, I was a rain forest. Despite toweling off and changing into clean professional wear of gauzy blouses and flowy skirts, I remained dewy the rest of the day, my hair appearing greased into its bun, a lingering smell of dirt that adhered to my sunscreened epidermis. The ride home was worse because it was in full sun. I was as toned and slim as a tween who'd just had her growth spurt, but as weak as a plucked string bean gone limp on the porch. Evenings were spent

working on my art portfolio and applications for design school before falling asleep and starting the commute all over again.

I think fondly back on that self, so desirous of more from life, so capable of evading lassitude. I was a serious adherent to my ambitions and passions, all so incomplete and enmeshed. It's not possible to extricate my motivation based on some idealized portrait of a future existence from my unadulterated emotions in any present activity. If I had paused for too long to reflect on whether I was making the "right" choices to optimize satisfaction, I might have become paralyzed in a never-doing. Instead, I sped toward my hypothetical dreams all at once as fiercely as my body would allow.

Early morning the e-mail comes: accepted to design (89) school in the UK with the scholarship I needed to go. One e-mail reroutes my entire motion. It's April. By October I will be gone, new home, new days. I jump on my bike for the commute to my final government job. A smile slices past my ears, streaking my hair, a gale whistling through my teeth. I become pneumatic tingles. My heart beats so strong it resounds as gong. I am flying. Only the bike can keep up with the exhilarated acceleration of my spirit.

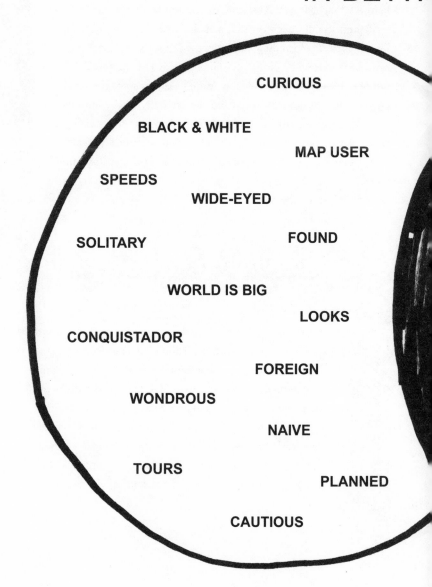

CURIOUS

BLACK & WHITE

MAP USER

SPEEDS

WIDE-EYED

SOLITARY

FOUND

WORLD IS BIG

LOOKS

CONQUISTADOR

FOREIGN

WONDROUS

NAIVE

TOURS

PLANNED

CAUTIOUS

NYNESS

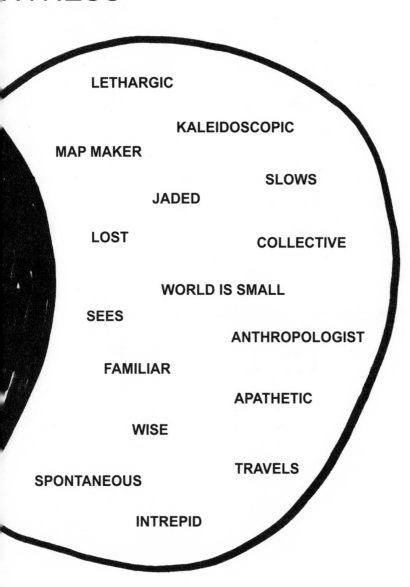

LETHARGIC

KALEIDOSCOPIC

MAP MAKER

SLOWS

JADED

LOST

COLLECTIVE

WORLD IS SMALL

SEES

ANTHROPOLOGIST

FAMILIAR

APATHETIC

WISE

TRAVELS

SPONTANEOUS

INTREPID

(91) In the Berenstain Bears' *The Bike Lesson*, Dad brings home a new bike. Dad gets on first to rhyme off lessons as Small Bear trails on foot awaiting his turn. With each lesson Dad attempts to model, Small Bear learns what not to do.[20]

> QUESTION: When approaching a puddle, do you go around or *ride right through*?
>
> ANSWER: Go around (Dad goes through).
>
> QUESTION: Before taking a road, what should you do?
>
> ANSWER: Know where *that road is going to go* (off a cliff Dad goes).
>
> QUESTION: Can you ever know where roads are going to go?
>
> QUESTION: Does knowing what to do secure the follow through?
>
> QUESTION: Yes or no?
>
> ANSWER:

(92) An ethics teacher once explained that when we think "bicycle," the picture that appears in our mind is an amalgam of the many bicycles we have encountered. It's an ideal that is averaged from a plural reality. The bicycle in my mind does not exist in the world, it is scrubbed of particularity, an impossible perfection. I wonder how many bicycles I needed to see before an image adhered to my mind's eye? Would one bicycle have sufficed? Would it have made for a more realistic standard? Could I have been happier believing only that one existed? How does that ideal image inform my judgment of future bicycles? How does that ideal change with every new bicycle I see? Does the world become more unified as I am exposed to its plurality? Does it fractal? Does it fray?

What happens when you are walking and cross paths with the shadow (93) of a passing bike? Do you shiver, sensing this spectral collision? Or does it provide a sudden boost in your speed, syncing with the flow of its revolutions?

Apparent movement is an optical illusion of perceived motion from (94) the inanimate. When staring at areas heavily patterned and of high-contrast lights and darks, the eye moves in rapid microsaccades and the visual appears to flicker. In the "Rotating Snakes" illusion, peripheral drift generates a constant sense of wheels moving clockwise and counterclockwise. If the eyes freeze their gaze at a single point, all motion halts.

(95)   I read an essay by Teju Cole writing about André Aciman writing about Claude Monet. I fasten myself to this spiral of writers writing about writers by writing about Cole's writing on Aciman's writing on Monet. In *Alibis: Essays on Elsewhere*, Aciman suggests Monet "liked painting this town more than he loved the town itself, because what he loved was more in him than in the town itself, though he needed the town to draw it out of him."[21] Cole notes that later in *Alibis*, Aciman describes his love of Rome similarly and that this leitmotif of Aciman's displays "his love of recursion and contradiction, of being 'elsewhere' . . . of cultivating shadow-selves and always feeling out of place. And, certainly, memory is nothing if not repetitive."[22] Scientists refer to our sixth sense being that of *proprioception*—the body's awareness of its position and ability to situate itself within an environment. In poet Charles Olson's poetic essay on the subject, there is the BODY, there is PLACE, and this third proprioceptive mid-thing, the SOUL, that acquires depth physically through "built-in space-time specifics," and this "*movement* or *action* is 'home.'"[23] It is my body creating friction and flow with external spaces that forges the self. And each time I fling, or am flung, into the foreign, my depurated essence recrystallizes.

DREAM BIKE QUESTIONNAIRE

TYPE

- ☐ fixed-gear
- ☒ hybrid
- ☐ BMX

- ☐ folding
- ☒ road
- ☒ cruiser

- ☐ cyclo-cross
- ☐ mountain

ACCESSORIES

- ☐ frame bag
- ☐ bottle cage

- ☒ mirrors
- ☒ bell

- ☒ basket
- ☒ lights

WHEEL SIZE

- ☐ 16"
- ☐ 20"
- ☐ 24"
- ☐ 26"
- ☒ 27.5"
- ☐ 29"
- ☐ 32"

HEIGHT

- ☐ 13-15"
- ☐ 15-16"
- ☐ 16-17"
- ☒ 17-19"

COST

- ☒ 0-100
- ☒ 100-300
- ☐ 300-750
- ▣ 750-2000
- ▣ 2000-3500
- ☐ 3500-6000
- ☐ 6000-10,000

↖ WTF???

COLOR

neon   ~~pastel~~   ~~brooding~~   metallic

(black)   red   blue

(white) ⟵ cream   orange   purple

silver   yellow   (pink) ⟵ pale or salmon or dirty

gold   mint or kelly (green) or forest   magenta ↑ NEVER AGAIN!!!

(turquoise)

My dream bike would be lightweight and compact with a front and back basket, a holster for my iPhone, fresh daisies or sunflowers between the handlebars, and a rust-free retro finish.

(97)   As spring approached, six months into my design studies at the University of Brighton, I finally bought a bike, my third bike purchase as an adult. Only a steep walk from where I lived was the weekend car boot sale at the Brighton Racecourse. A car boot sale is like a garage sale, only better because it happens every weekend, and instead of one person selling things from their garage, hundreds of people are selling things from their trunks ("boots") all in one place. There was a man who brought a large collection of cheap used bicycles each weekend. It was difficult to properly test a bike in the packed field, but I was so impatient, I bought the one the man insisted was my size. Immediately upon dangerously speeding down the hill, I realized my mistake. The bike was oversized enough that when on the seat, I had to extend my toes to graze the gravel, not able to dismount firmly because of the high horizontal crossbar. I hadn't realized the distinction between men's and women's bikes. Historically, women's bikes had a slanted crossbar so that they could gracefully swing their leg over in a dress, while the horizontal crossbar was used to reinforce the strength of the frame, which was preferable for the rigorous riding of men compared with the dainty dillydally of women. Modern materials now allow a slanted frame to suffice. Dress-clad or not, I can't see why men or women would prefer the horizontal crossbar impediment. I tipped over outside my house and called the number on the bike man's business card. He agreed to allow me to exchange it for a smaller bike that he would bring to next week's car boot sale.

FERRIS WHEEL

My fourth bicycle was a teal mountain bike. It was a Sunday afternoon (98) in March, the sun was refulgent, and the sky and sea wore matching azures. I rode my bike down from the car boot sale overlooking the colorful terraced homes sloping toward the pebbled beach. To my right was the Brighton Wheel and Pier by all the shops, work, and school buildings I frequented daily. To my left was terra incognita. I turned left and rode adjacent the seafront promenade, passing the marina as beach gave way to cliffside. Below was chalky escarpment and thrashing waves becoming rainbow mist becoming waves again. I was on a grassy headland with an eternity of ocean splaying out all around. Soon appeared a green mound topped with a smock mill. I dropped my bike near the mill and lay starfished in the grass. Between the curvature of the mound and the uninterrupted seascape, I felt Earth's rotundity. As breathtaking as the ocean was, it was the grass that startled me now. Brighton is compact, alleyways and boxed-in gardens clinging to where human land ends and unfathomable blue begins. Not since departing Canada had I potted myself amidst so much green. This was the nature of my childhood. I had forgotten the feeling of being anchored by terra firma, where a pounding heart is found in my ears and I swear my body is tracking the spinning planet.

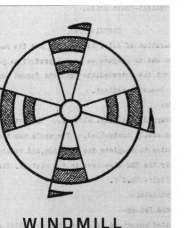

WINDMILL

(99)   I went to Amsterdam to visit Sailor, who was studying there for a semester. We biked to Kersenbloesempark, where four hundred cherry blossom trees, gifted by the Japanese, were planted in a circle. The grove forms a flowering canopy under which people picnic and play. It was April, so the blossoms had turned white, with petals wafting down like snow. The day we were there, a film crew was shooting a commercial with a white horse, which only added to the ethereal tableau. We lay on a blanket with stroopwafels and music, while we wrote and read and monologued confessions. In Japanese, the word *komorebi* translates to a scattered sunlight that passes through leaves of trees. It kind of makes the world glitter in slow motion. My twenties felt this way. The aesthetics of a setting have always elevated my spiritual attentiveness. To what extent that glitter can or should be prioritized and maintained as I age and settle remains a teetering question in my mind.

(100)   In Amsterdam, bicycles reign, so much so that some streets permit only bicycles. The city ranks as one of the top five most bike-friendly cities in the world. Bicycles are estimated to outnumber residents. They populate every scene. There are bike traffic jams and bike traffic accidents, but there are also many streets that are unpopulated. Thousands of bicycles are packed like a warehouse of sardines by the train station. Bicycles are parked against bridges and outside every shop.

    The most common crime in Amsterdam is bike theft. As a result, many Dutch bikes have a ring lock built into their rear wheel. The key stays in the lock while you ride, and when you need to stop for an errand, you can quickly remove it and leave your bike freestanding with the assurance that any thief would have to conspicuously drag the bike away. We rented bikes to cover the city's concentric streets separated by canals, joined by bridges, and lined by tall *grachtenpanden* with their distinctive stepped roofs, earth-toned façades, and white-trimmed gridded windows. I loved Amsterdam's picturesque neatness, its com-

pact waterway openness, and its absence of cars—hideously obtrusive pollutants of my inner peace; machines incongruent with the breath of the living. However, it was on this trip that I began to dismantle visions of long-term residency in Europe. It was a fairy tale without bloodlines to my language, culture, or people, which I was coming to suspect were essential scaffolding to my architecture.

(101) In suburban childhood, when we were done on our bikes, we could smash them down in the front lawn or driveway or any old place we pleased and stomp on into the house or off to play without threat that they wouldn't be there patiently awaiting our return. The bikes were not a thief's commodity; they were ours like a worn pair of shoes shaped to our foot's print.

(102) I au-paired in Bologna for a five-year-old boy named Jacopo. The family lived near the Piazza Maggiore in the romantic Old Town. Jacopo spoke no English; I, no Italian. Days were challenging, tedious, and packed with physically and visually stimulating activities: science experiments, making a life-sized paper skeleton with all the bones in the body labeled in English, terrariums for garden bugs, crafts, baked goods, edible crafts and crafty baked goods, and visits to museums, libraries, and parks via bicycle (though he probably would have been happier watching *Minions* on repeat all of every day). Jacopo was a thick and spoiled boy who still sat in a seat behind a parent on their bike. Hoisting him onto this seat while straddling the kickstand-less bike was a daunting test of strength. Once we fell over in the process and I thought he might never trust me again. But then a day later I saved him from being hit by a car and all faith was restored. To fill time, I would take him on curly rides around the cobblestone alleys and squares of the medieval center. We never took a direct route anywhere (not that I would have known one), allowing me to get lost exploring while he nodded off in frustration over my aimlessness. For this brief

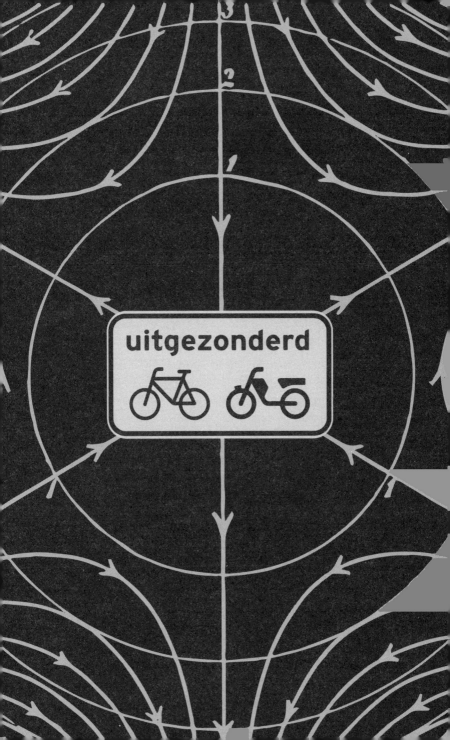

time, I sampled the idyll of stereotypical European life, but strangely that's not what I came to lust over.

Jacopo's parents had him in their early forties after establishing their lives in academia and investing in a loving intelligentsia. Most dinners, we were joined on the terrace by friends who leisurely stayed for wine and laughter into the night. I accompanied them to weddings, friend beach weekends, and grandparents' homes in the Emilia-Romagna countryside. Time floated here—loitering in moonlight eating gelato, conversing with passersby in the streets, shuffling through markets, and preparing and eating meals. Simple basics were ritualized and concretized between a clan sharing intention and *gioia di vivere*. It was the exemplification of *belonging*, the belonging of and with others.

(103)   I watched *Wadjda*, the first film to be shot entirely in Saudi Arabia and the first feature film made by a female Saudi director. The film follows ten-year-old Wadjda trying to earn enough money to buy a bicycle. There is so much stifling tension and lack of freedom that builds with every failed attempt to get closer to her goal. It's a ninety-eight-minute capsule of desire. In the final scene, she wobbly-races her best male friend down a dusty road. "Catch me if you can," she says, closing the film with a breathy smile and a victorious stare off into the distance. Saudi women were prohibited from riding bicycles in public until 2013 (the year after the film was released), when the government eased restrictions to allow for chaperoned recreational cycling.

(104)   My teal bicycle had been bequeathed to a classmate over the summer. I returned to discover she had abandoned it on a street pole, vacated to another part of town, and sealed its stolen fate.

(105)   Back to the car-boot-sale bike man for my fifth bicycle—an orange mountain bike. It lived a rough life outside my town house, being eroded by English rains and salty seaside air. I used it every day to

bike to class, to multiple jobs, to grocery shopping, to the pool, for beach rides, and to the train station on days I commuted to London for internships. Nothing was farther than fifteen minutes along the ocean. My world was small, but oh so spry and carbonated.

I brought my bike on the train into London to spend my birthday (106) with my friend Peretz. We had met in Bangladesh. There was a kinship to how our hearts raced pondering our place in life. He was the first person I wanted to couple with. I loved the possibility of him. I would say yes to anything when we were together. He was an avid cyclist, going on group cycle trips across Europe and commuting exclusively by bike wherever he was based. His days were structured like boxes on a perpetual bucket list thirsting for checkmarks. Early morning, I rode from the London station to the boathouse, where we kayaked on the Thames. We rode to his house for lunch, then loaded our bikes on the tube to debark in the center. We only rode for a few minutes before Peretz's bike chain broke. We locked up our bikes and went by foot for a jaunt through the British Museum, then an hour north to the neon sign warehouse God's Own Junkyard. Electric-magenta haze with exclamatory words screamed out. It was hypnagogic sitting with him on the vinyl sofa tucked under the vibrating signs THRILLS, LOVE, and THE BRIGHT & THE SHINY as bluegrass twanged. We talked deeply over Bengali food on Brick Lane before retrieving our bikes. At the tube station, he was readying to board a train going one way, me the other. After three years and escapades in four countries, I told him that I *liked* him (even though I actually thought I *loved* him). He ran with his bike to catch his train. That was the last time we shared the same physical space. We've spoken since, but I can never go back to that dreamlike space of suspended hope of something more.

2 8 FEB 2015

HOVE → 7:05 AM → BRIGHTON STATION

PUTNEY BRIDGE

CLAPHAM JUNCTION

PUTNEY BRIDGE

Sarno Arms Boathouse

PUTNEY ← BRIDGE

PUTNEY BRIDGE

SHEPHERDS BUSH

lunch at Jessie's

SHEPHERDS BUSH

British Museum

KING'S CROSS

BRICK LANE

Bengali Dinner + Shaheed Minar memorial

ALDGATE

KING'S CROSS

BRIGHTON

HOME 1:35 AM

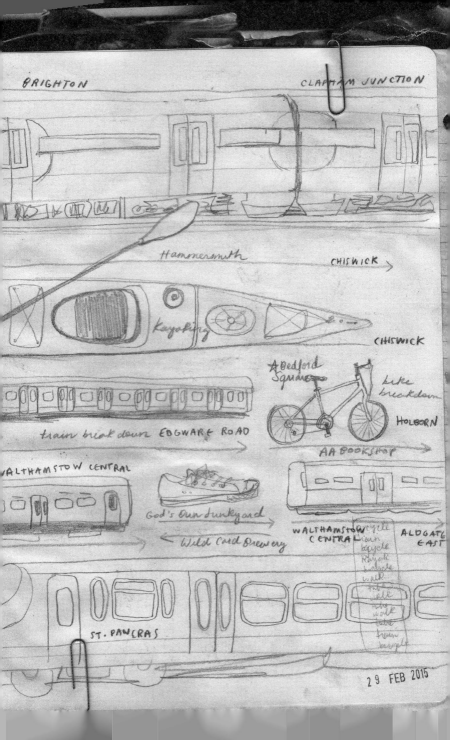

BRIGHTON

CLAPHAM JUNCTION

Hammersmith

CHISWICK →

Kayaking

CHISWICK

A Bedford Square

bike breakdown

HOLBORN

train break down EDGWARE ROAD

AA BOOKSHOP →

WALTHAMSTOW CENTRAL

God's Own Junkyard →

← Wild Card Brewery

WALTHAMSTOW CENTRAL

bicycle train
bicycle
kayak
bike
walk
tube
dog walk
tube
train
bicycle

ALDGATE EAST

ST. PANCRAS

2 9 FEB 2015

(107) In the port city of Essaouira, I am rambling alone when a beautiful Moroccan boy about my age strolls by with a fancy green bicycle. He has an Afro blowout, white Ray-Bans and tank top, and a surfer vibe. He felt wide-open giddy. I followed him home, into an old *riad* off a sunny alley. Looking up from the interior courtyard were Moorish balconies with worn shutters, walls of aging layers of paint, and midday bright beaming through the mosaic glass ceiling. Looking down were guitars laid on a low carved wooden table. I could see into the ground-floor bedrooms with graffiti murals, rugged bohemian textiles, and surf- and skateboards leaning against the walls. Two of his friends were sitting there, one apparently the best Moroccan player of the Beatles' music. I sat down, and he went over to a fancy stereo and put on "Blackbird." My stomach filled with fireflies. That was my song. My go-to when locals requested I sing to them (this sounds absurd, but it occurred in many countries I visited, much to their disappointment).

I always feel like I am waiting to fall into an effortless whirlwind romantic comedy. I wish I could tell you what followed was greeting camels on the beach at sunset, with windsurfers in the distance; a night out dancing followed by an early morning of sex and breakfast on the roof; and a return to my hotel on the back of his green bicycle. That fantasy could have unfurled had I not been so scared and so safe. I stayed for a bit, we exchanged numbers, I reunited with my friends, he called in the night after I was already tucked in bed. I wasn't ready to be uninhibited and promiscuous, maybe I never will be. I wanted my body to naturally melt into his with flaming desire, but I was frozen stiff. I want these spontaneous exploits, but then I lean back into controlled activities. Maybe I want to only collect, but not actually sit long in, such experiences. I say I want to get lost in someone else's story, but I never do.

My friend Frida and I went backpacking through Romania for three (108) weeks. Like most of my travels pre-smartphone technology, in my pocket I kept paper maps of each locale I would visit that I had screen-shotted close-ups of from Google Maps, painstakingly stitched together on Photoshop, printed out tabloid-sized, and starred with every place of personal interest: museums and galleries; lookout points at sunset; live music venues; theaters with notable shows; shipyards; hiking spots; artisan shops; bus stops; train stations; flea markets; food markets; textile markets; camel markets; witches' markets; tribal market days; architectural feats; rock-hewn churches; muralled mosques; old librar-ies; thermal baths; salt flats; a lobby with an elaborately tiled floor or fish tank or cathedral ceiling; the largest stupa; the Widest Tree in the World; a terra-cotta house; a neon sign graveyard; a geotagged photo suggesting a wall with a banyan tree growing through it, an unmarked pottery village, a shore with wild horses, a field of mustard flowers; a rumored corner where a blog claimed a man would wait to take you to a rooftop overlooking a tannery or an old woman would wait to bring you into her cave filled with locks of hair, etc. Of course, en route to locate any of these stars would lead to tangential discoveries never marked or mentioned online, or the star would correspond to nothing but I would have spent the whole day looking, detoured by welcoming locals who would invite me in for rose jam and bread dipped in oil and za'atar or a performance with their *davul*, or have me hold their baby or talk to their toddler in English or take a picture with their oldest family member, or paint a watercolor with saffron, or have my hand hennaed or my face powdered with color. I would end up stumbling upon a silk-screening studio or a flower farm or tropical poinsettia covered in butterflies or a wake of vultures feeding on topi or a shoe-lace factory or ritual dance ceremony or most often a tiny vignette of ongoings and light and layers of time all congregating into a moment for me to see then gone in the squall that is the motion of life.

Frida and I visited some sleepy Transylvanian villages via bicycle that seemed clustered near one another in a way that was convenient for tour buses but not expedient via public bus. We boarded a train with our borrowed bikes, mine too small, Frida's too big and broken. Our guesthouse had told us the name of the station where we needed to debark, how long it would take, and how many stops to wait. At our supposed destination, the doors swung open at an empty ditch of prickly weeds. We should have waited, but instead, without a smartphone GPS, we ran. I threw my bike out, leaped eight feet down, and dragged it out of the way so Frida could do the same. We walked for ten minutes over the tracks to the abandoned station, which was the intended destination to begin our day of cycling.

At the age of twenty-five, I was grappling with my sexuality, nearing the end of my UK degree, and hovering in not knowing how or where I should be. We did so much in Romania, but mostly, Frida and I reminisce over the hilarity of our bike journey. We remember returning to the correct station at the end of the day, which was empty, three of four platforms under construction. A worker helped hoist our bikes over the flatbed cars that were blocking our way to the farthest and only functioning rail, where a late train of two cars would eventually stop, to our great relief. Though travel was no longer central to my life, the unexpected detours, laughter breaking a cry, the scour for stars . . . still offered recesses from my times of grief.

I CouchSurfed for the first time in Barcelona. My host was eager for the company, being an exchange student from Poland. She invited me to accompany her to Museu Nacional d'Art de Catalunya. It is awkward visiting a museum with a stranger, having to moderate one's pace to respect someone else's curiosity and contemplativeness. I took one photo while there of a Ramon Casas i Carbó painting: *Ramon Casas and Pere Romeu on a Tandem* (1897). Casas made it to hang in Romeu's new modernist bar, Els Quatre Gats. An inscription scrawled in the corner of the original painting that has since been removed read, in Catalan, "To ride a bicycle, you can't have a straight back", which nodded to Romeu's attitude about tradition being an obstacle to progress. In true modernist fashion, the painting was replaced with *Ramon Casas and Pere Romeu in an Automobile* (1901) to beckon the dawn of a new century. (109)

I have never ridden a tandem bicycle. I wonder if it is harder or easier to ride it alone.

(110)   There are some countries where
        I have no memories of bicycles,
        until I return to travel photos
        and it is like a *Where's Waldo?*
        of bikes creeping into shots.

(111) And there other countries where bikes were like gleaming jewels in my photographs, despite not riding them. I didn't ride a bicycle in Aveiro, even though bicycles were freely available. I didn't ride in Dar es Salaam, despite having booked a bike tour. I didn't ride in Cappadocia, even though my itinerary suggested so. I didn't ride in Egypt—too hot. Nor Bolivia—no oxygen. Not in Mexico or Hungary or Madagascar (I had never planned to). I don't consider any of these instances to be failures to freewheel; in fact, it was the opposite. It was in these places that I allowed others to decide our turns, to practice releasing control and inviting a collective wonder that is birthed by people rather than place.

(112)   My friend Easton and I began research for a series of whimsical guides
        of London. On weekends, we would gallivant around a borough doc-
        umenting hidden gems and gathering ephemera. We snuck into posh
        hotels, inquired at secret societies, toured cemeteries, sampled food and
        drink, dug through vintage boutiques, and sat sketching cross-legged
        on floors. Once we used bicycles to Easton's dismay (she was a slug-
        gish, nervous cycler), but mostly we walked. We called our project the
        Dérivist Guides, taken from Guy Debord's psychogeographic theory of
        the *dérive*.[24] The theory posits that our typical movement through the
        world is so narrowly planned that we overlook its layered details. It
        encourages spontaneously moving through the ambiences of an urban
        terrain, allowing encounters along the way to direct one's journey in
        order to rouse new perspectives and connect with the soul of a place.
        Debord believed that while one could do this alone, results were better
        when done in multiple small groups that could coalesce revelations.
        Easton and I never got past the research stage.

(113)   Of the 234 bottle caps I have plucked off the ground in thirty coun-
        tries over the last twenty years, only two have a bicycle on them, New
        Belgium Brewing in orange (LEFT) and red (RIGHT).

My orange bike broke mid-shift at my summer job as a youth leader (114) for an international language camp. On my lunch break, I walked to the nearest bike shop and was told it would be cheaper to buy a new one than replace the odd old part. I left with the cheapest used bike they had—my sixth bicycle and prettiest yet, a purple cruiser—and sped back up along the beach to entertain tweens. The upright bike was perfect for elegant small-town moving and shaking.

In springtime as a child, when the balding schoolyard was thawing dark grass and deltas of melting ice, in my peacoat and school uniform, I would impersonate a prim lassie walking through British countryside. My eyes would overlay every prosaic scene with an illusion of quaint character. I wanted to live in relics of past ornament, where bewitchery percolated through the floorboards and wallpaper seams and patina coatings that were whispering witnesses to yore.

In Brighton, this winsomeness existed all around me without any maladaptive daydreaming. Art students dressed like grunge teenagers with analog cameras around their necks and sketchbooks spilling from their leather satchels. Pubs were staged with velvet armchairs, covered with antique oil paintings of dead white guys, and haunted by nineteenth-century century literary ghosts. Buskers not becoming James Bay or Passenger crooned and strummed, soloed on violins or saxophones or watchamacallits. Parks were wildly overgrown, there were swans in ponds, rose bushes, cafés serving tea and small sandwiches. My room had fifteen-foot ceilings, a fireplace, and a view of a spiral staircase in a garden courtyard. I woke to a soft light and the sound of seagulls. I stepped outside to the same ocean horizon each day, only it never looked the same. I rode my bike through lanes of Victorian buildings past the Indo-Saracenic-styled Royal Pavilion, stopping at the art or antique shop for supplies. Days were spent on design experiments; nights were spent shelving books in the library. The weather was amenable to biking year-round, though everything local was walkable, everything national was trainable, everything continental was Ryanair-able.

(115)   In Scotland, I retreated into farmwork on a Hare Krishna compound. There was one devotee who walked around a tiled circle in the garden all day, chanting his mantra on a *japamala*. I understood this to be like praying the rosary, which I did only during school Masses in sixth grade after Pope John Paul II declared it "the Year of the Rosary." A verse is recited, resets, and repeats until the tongue senses no beginning or end to the verse or any one word, spaces between letters close up, and a slurred song replaces all thought. A circle of beads helps the fingers enumerate the repetitions in Christianity, Buddhism, Hinduism, Islam, Jainism, and Sikhism. Does time move fast or slow in a trance? Which I would prefer depends on the day. Maybe if one stays entranced long enough, all time reveals itself to be, as Friedrich Nietzsche hypothesized, eternally recurrent—"life as you now live it and have lived it, you will have to live once more and innumerable times more; and there will be nothing new in it, but every pain and every joy and every thought and sigh and everything unutterably small or great in your life will have to return to you."[25] And once this cyclical truth is realized, "how well disposed would you have to become to yourself and to life to crave nothing more fervently than this ultimate eternal confirmation and seal?"[26] When I watched that devotee I didn't feel reverent, I felt sad. What had happened to make him want to tighten his recurrence to the size of a verse? Then again, what had happened to make me want to dilate mine to unapparent ends?

(116)   In geometry, a circle is the outer boundary of a disc without eccentricities and with coincident foci. The bull's-eye is equidistant from all escape routes off the round; but with angularity studies confirming the human eye's strong preference for the curvilinear, one is unlikely to wish escape from shapely perfection. Perhaps we are lured by the circle because it represents emoticons of feeling and connection—other human faces, of our home planet, or the source of energy, light, and our sight. Manuel Lima's *The Book of Circles* traces humankind's pro-

pensity for drawing circles back forty thousand years to petroglyphs, then later, mandalas.[27]

In Tantrism, mandalas are like bowls holding the forces of the cosmos. The Sanskrit verse *Yat pinde tat brahmande* means "all that is outside you is within you," the microcosm of the self is equal to the macrocosm of the universe. With ornately illustrated radial symmetry, mandalas are architected to assist with our awareness and strengthening of this umbilical cord through inducing the mind toward its center—similar to how multidisciplinary artist Jenny Odell describes walking a circular labyrinth enables a "sort of dense infolding of attention."[28]

During World War II, Carl Jung sketched a mandala every day, believing the,

> severe pattern imposed by a circular image of this kind compensates the disorder and confusion of the psychic state—namely, through the construction of a central point to which everything is related, or by a concentric arrangement of the disordered multiplicity and of contradictory and irreconcilable elements . . . [It is] an attempt at self-healing on the part of Nature, which does not spring from conscious reflection but from an instinctive impulse.[29]

This means orbital realignment could be possible right now, or now, or now. I could stare into a mandala, or sketch one, or close my eyes and imagine, like a Wiccan casting a magic circle on the ground in salt, that I am standing at a center of power, a Hula-Hoop-sized universe where chaos is small and controlled. I have brief moments, at least twice a day, where I am stilled in this concentrated discoid. Sometimes I can waft in the storm's eye long enough that it might take a few hours or a few days before, again, chaos overtakes. It will overtake. And there are times when life breaks my heart and I can't summon the circle at all. Monthly someone suggests I should meditate, but I don't, not officially.

JAPAMALA 108 Beads
(Sikkim, Buddhism, Jainism, Hinduism)

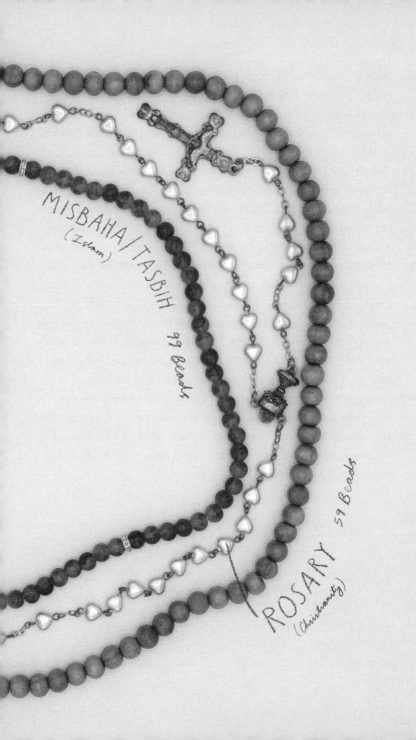

MISBAHA/TASBIH
(Islam)

99 Beads

ROSARY
(Christianity)

59 Beads

(117)   I don't remember what became of my last bicycle in the UK, that purple cruiser. Did I gift it to a friend? Leave it locked outside my Regency town house two blocks from the sea? Sell it? No way, I never got around to that sort of thing. I would have kept it until the final moment.

(118)   Every place I had been before New York City felt destined for transience in my search for a permanent home. Landing grounds were treated as launch pads. Then came New York and I couldn't see a life beyond it. I loved its presence and I loved its potential futures. I bought my seventh bike exactly seven months into living in Brooklyn. I found a vintage Schwinn Suburban on Craigslist for $130. The owner said it might need new brakes or tires, but it was sky blue and stylish and I wanted it. The nearest bike shop certified it was in perfect working order, made of Chicago steel (which made it mighty durable but also mighty heavy). I installed a bike basket large enough to load a week's worth of groceries and bought a bell and lights and the highest-rated lock on Amazon. It had been too long since I had ridden, maybe the longest stretch I had gone since the two years from birth to that trailer park trike. On my ride home, cautiousness soon gave way to the familiar exaltation that comes with each mount, wherein I am greeted by an immutable cast of myself forged out of glass and whatever liquid swirled with opal flecks fills a snow globe.

- EXCERPTED TRANSCRIPT -

[00:00:00]

TA: Hi! Can you hear me?

AW: Yes!

TA: Okay, let's talk bicycles.

AW: Fun. I love meditating about bikes.

TA: What is your earliest memory of a bike?

AW: Hmmm, my grandfather, who died when he was ninety-three or ninety-seven, would wake up every day at 5:00 AM and bike to get fresh baked goods for breakfast, pretty much until he died.

TA: Would you watch and wait for him to arrive?

AW: I would see him coming back. Also, we talked about it a lot because nobody else from the family was so active or cared about biking as much . . . and having him be so fit at his age, people were amazed.

[00:08:30]

TA: What's the longest you've ever biked without stopping? Like, longest continuous ride.

AW: There were some pretty long days when I did my three-week bikepacking art project. I've biked a hundred miles in a day. It took the whole day, for sure, but it's not as intense as it sounds.

TA: I imagine, like some other forms of exercise, there's a period when you're wondering "When is this going to end?" and then if you pass that point, you are so in it that you could keep going forever.

AW: Usually the tiredness hits only when I stop, but when I'm moving, I don't feel it.

TA: In your dream reality, where your life is exactly balanced the way you want it to be, how much of your day would be spent on a bike?

AW: Oh my God. If I could pick . . . most of it. I don't think I'm a person that would compete, but whatever, bikepacking, leading bike tours across something . . .

TA: So why not make that your profession? Maybe you wouldn't love it as much if it was your livelihood . . .

AW: Yeah, I wonder if I would get bored of it, I don't know if I have biked for long enough in my life to be able to judge, but it's the one thing that I haven't gotten bored of. My personality and my system demand so much stimulation and biking really gets me with that. And the landscape all around. It regulates. It's highly regulating, I think. And when you are a regulated being, you can show up the best for people, which ultimately is what makes me happy.

[00:16:30]

TA: What's one of the single best rides of your life?

AW: That's hard. A couple years ago, there was a time where bikes kind of brought me back to life and back to feeling like myself. I remember having these night rides after 2:00 AM where the city was completely vacant. A weird hour after people who'd partied had gone home, but early commuters were not yet out. The city would often have this night or morning mist, and lights would kind of reflect off the pavement in beautiful colors, and the city was just, like, mine. I would play music and dance on the bike.

TA: How do you dance on a bike?

AW: It's more like dancing with the bike. Leaning with my body, swerving side to side.

TA: As if you and your bike are one?

AW: Exactly. Bike dancing should have its own word. And I wish we could, like, unite around that word. I need that.

TA: It should have its own category because you're not riding along a path, you're sort of swerving and improvising?

AW: Yeah. And it feels—I don't know if it looks—but it feels much more elegant. It doesn't feel like a sport. It feels like an art. And there's no wrong way to do it. I guess there is more freedom of expression when it's just your body on a dance floor, but the speed is a whole different thing. Ideally I am bike dancing in an open plain and can see everything around me, the nature moving past.

[00:36:30]

TA: If you close your eyes and imagine a snapshot of yourself on a bike, what does that picture look like?

AW: That's a good question. It is me on my old bike, actually, a bike that got stolen. I'm a few years younger and on the bridge that crosses to the Rockaways, at this specific spot when you see all the water that's ahead, all the beaches and inlets and the fishermen, and the wind is blowing in your face, but it's not overwhelming . . .
The Rockaways is the best ride a cyclist can take in New York City. When people ask me to take them on a ride and it's too windy to go there, I am so lost.

TA: Absolutely, that ride has my heart. It was my first in the city.

AW: Oh my God. What a ride to pick.

My first New York bike ride was to the Rockaways. I rode for over (120) an hour through suburban Ditmas Park with its old porches and lawns—down Neptune Avenue, which felt like a fishing village—over the Marine Parkway Bridge with views of tiny waterfront homes— through Fort Tilden's fields—then into a thick forested maze that lacerated and itched at my skin until eventually opening onto beach. For another hour, I walked barefoot with my bike by the edge of the water, passing the odd couple or fishing pole. Then I *arrived*. I hadn't known my destination until I got there. Breezy Point Tip. All around was powder-blue water fading into cloudless sky. To one side was where I had walked from, now a misty distance. Inland were grassy dunes that rose up high enough to obstruct any sight of human-made life, like a dream sequence of heaven in one's mind. My body was thirsty and weak and finally permitted glorifying release. I could hear only wind greeting water as I waded out knee-deep into the ocean and took a bite of my chilled peanut butter and banana sandwich. I felt baptized by New York, far from everything but who I was in this nearly gone minute, eating what I have since dubbed my best meal.

(121) I eventually settled in Park Slope, joining three women in the top three floors of an old Kinko-style row house three blocks from Prospect Park. I would bike down the tree-lined streets for errands to specialty grocers and thrift shops, the farmers market, the hardware store; my bike basket filled with a baguette, a bouquet, a vintage find, foreign confections, supplies for festooning or table setting, an obscure ingredient needed for an elaborate recipe. Everything was nearby, everything appeared nice, all the pieces enabling my entrancement into the co-creation and maintenance of our picturesque haven. The house was massive; there was an unobstructed view of the Manhattan skyline from our private roof and charm creaking like a fiddle from every wooden step. As we became acquainted, we progressively injected more and more hygge into the space. We called ourselves the House of Little Women, all there growing up and into ourselves, moving between being friends, sisters, mothers, therapists, comedians, storytellers, teachers, students, hype girls. We took turns dealing with mice, cockroaches, leaks, and our inner clean freaks. We watched films on a projector, gave PowerPoint presentations, helped review job applications, swapped clothes, braided hair, sewed, weaved, danced, watered plants, built forts, stuffed stockings, played records, painted nails, led yoga sessions. We debated the best Taylor Swift song, the boringest story, the cheapest grocery stores, the most soothing ASMR sound, the flat's feng shui, the goings-on of our neighbors heard through windows. We invested in midcentury furniture, populated shelves with quirky stoop finds, made art for the walls, and had a bulging closet of decorations for holidays and celebrations. We would host dinner parties, concerts, craft nights, and any other gathering one could conceive. We baked and mixed cocktails and ordered takeout and put the kettle on for tea. We were there for one another in big and small ways. A for-now family. The first place that showed me the potential of home. I fell in love there, with the people and the place and the integral part I played in it all.

(122) Carrying a heavy bike down the three sharp-turning flights of my house's stairs veers into near-death act. My clothes permanently sport bike chain grease. My back hates me.

(123) Once on her daily bike commute from her home in Washington Square Park to our office near Times Square, my boss's arm was broken while she was stopped at a red light as another cyclist plowed into her and onward through the red.

(124) I mostly don't wear my helmet. I know this is bad. I feel your head shakes and judging glares. You are whisking this book from your impressionable children's hands. You are recycling this book or asking for a refund at your local indie bookstore or requesting the library ban it. You are writing a one-star review about how you wish zero stars were permissible. If my ride consists of navigating many busy non-bike-lane streets for an extended period, I will wear it. But mostly, I don't. Maybe admitting this vice will shame me into doing better.

(125) When I think of helmets, I have a nostalgic sensation of one being placed on my head; the buckle carefully snapped under my chin to avoid pinching skin—which happened enough times (or only once) that the lead-up would cause me to brace in a wince (because for children, one time is enough to devise a pattern of distrust); then the strap tightening more than I would like; and a hand palming the helmet's top, now one with my skull, rocking us in a motion of "yes" "no." The sensation is Dad before childhood bike rides. It's been more than twenty-five years, but that habitude is embedded into my body's memory. I understood exactly how Dad's weight translated into his resting arm pushing the Velcro foam against my hair, how far his bony fingers extended over the plastic shell, how I leaned into his torso knowing his cologne, knowing his body temperature, without having to look to verify his identity. That kind of closeness is tribal. It installs a homing

140

device inside our guts. And then we grow up, maybe we go away, left craving that closeness once again, in a friend-partner-child. Eventually we becoming the bestower of such tribal feelings to another.

On a plane, I drift in and out of watching scenes from the Mexican (126) rom-com *Everybody Loves Somebody*. Two ex-lovers ride bikes down a steep cliff in Baja California.

DANIEL

You're my first home.

CLARA

Exactly ... We always leave our first home.

Later a scene with a married couple distills the truest home I will come to seek.

ABBY

Can you breathe when you're not with me? ...
Do you think we've ever been in love? ...

    [MAX takes ABBY's hand and points to a freckle]

MAX

This wasn't here two months ago.

ABBY

Because I'm getting old! This is an old lady hand
freckle! You're not helping.

MAX

I'm saying that it's new. I know every inch of you,
but you remain surprising. I notice every tiny change
because I'm here to notice. My purpose in life is to
keep track of you ... that's love. I can breathe
without you just fine. What would be the point?[30]

141

(127) I am in a studio collaborating with woodworking friend Radcliffe to build a coffee table. We start late; he is first helping a cannabis courier make a wooden cup, which has proven difficult. The courier is convinced that his work will be substantially swifter and lighter if he carries a wooden cup rather than a water bottle and simply asks customers to refill it with every delivery. I can't explain why a plastic cup wouldn't have sufficed, or really any number of other lightweight drink containers, but maybe these are insider secrets traded only between cycling drug couriers. Radcliffe narrates every step in his carpentry process to me; it all sounds like a metaphor for living . . . Mathematical exactitude of measurements cannot be executed perfectly by the hand's tools against nature's wood. But wood is forgiving of human error. A bit of whittling, sanding, and rejigging and pieces will find their fit. *You see, we are dealing with imperceptible quantities.* Yes, the table is a big solid thing from a once bigger tree, but it is chips, curls, flakes, slivers, wafers, flour, wool, shavings, and dust—tree particles. But I can't yet see this Tree of fitted things; I see just aerosols drifting, dithering.

(128) For the first time in years, I find my way back to farmwork in Connecticut. By 6:00 AM each morning, I'm cutting flowers from the fields, picking berries, and harvesting every sort of vegetable. I read and wrote on the porch midday, collected eggs from the chicken coop in the afternoon, joined the family for dinner, strolled the shoreline in moonlight, slept early, and awoke to begin the cycle all over again.

Behind the barn was a graveyard of bikes all equally abused by weather and time. I fit a rusty old single-speed cruiser with foam bulging from the seat, a skittish coaster brake, and a wobbly balloon tire that resisted straight paths and hugged tight to turns. I would ride it trepidly around to fawn over the wealthy estates and town charm or down to the beach for a quick float between chores. The stay felt like a sort of therapeutic sensory deprivation: Days were this—sixteen hours of fresh air—a small bag of clothes to wear—simple meals—company

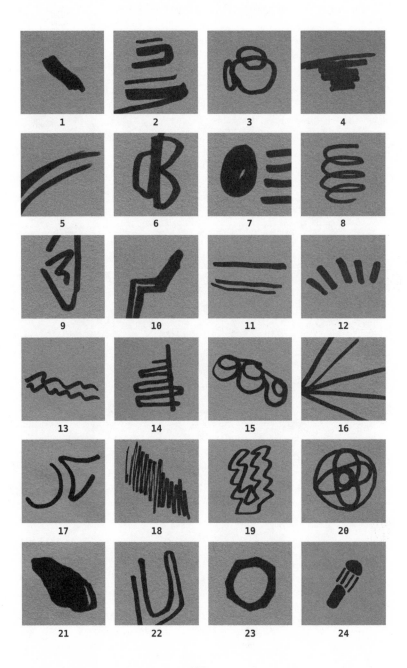

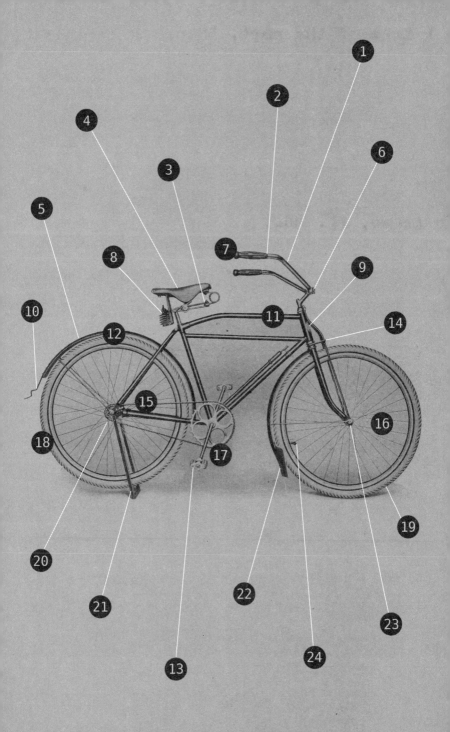

of the family and local labor straddling careers. I began squirmish, my mind compulsively reeling in attempts to productively populate my time with projects, excursions, and goal-oriented learning. But soon, I let go and nestled into the sounds of birds and rustling leaves and the feeling of dirt and sea. I was free from inundating choices that I might fail to capitalize on, free from trying to analyze my social capital: measuring out the weight of who I was loving and how much and what of it I got back.

After ten days, a tropical storm made its way to us. The father and son invited me to go see the waves. I thought we'd walk the ten minutes across the road, but they said to grab my bike. On the beach, the usually still ocean was waves upon waves looking like abalone shells, somersaulting open from their chalky, corrugated outsides to their nacreous insides. There were seagulls flying backward. A capsized sailboat. No one but us. It was safer to stand in the froth of tumultuous waters than on solid ground because the sand pelted the skin with a million microscopic Tasers. The father stretched his arms like an albatross and glided through the water and up over a dune, following the changing winds that pulled taut his dirt-stained khakis, taupe button-down, and suntanned wrinkly face that was flushed giddy. I saw him transform to boy. The path leading back to the farm was blocked by fallen trees, so I detoured through the grassy field. The winds rolling off the coast followed me, pushed me forward. I flashed back to Daryl that first day riding training wheel–less. I felt transformed to girl. When we returned, the electricity was gone and remained gone for the rest of my stay, which only dug me further into ataraxia. We played board games by candlelight. We played ultimate Frisbee. We spent hours picking up sticks strewn by the storm. By the end, I was dreading the return to city life. But I couldn't stay. I had to go back to claim what could be mine. The family said I was welcome any time, and for once I left something vowing no more final goodbyes.

(129) When I am drowsy but not ready for sleep to jolt me into tomorrow, I rewatch the opening monologues from the years that Tina Fey and Amy Poehler hosted the Golden Globes. In 2015's, Poehler joked that Wes Anderson arrived at the awards on "a homemade bicycle made of antique tuba parts." I didn't laugh or get it, but now whenever I think of tubas, I picture them in the shape of a bike being ridden by Anderson.

(130) A compilation video in my head of bicycle footage from television and film begins with *Friends*'s Ross bracing Phoebe in her first stiff moments on a bike / cut to a close-up frontal shot of a character pumping slaphappy / a paperboy tossing newspapers in the vague vicinity of porches (*see* opening scene of *Barb and Star Go to Vista Del Mar*) / a view from the rider's perspective over the handlebars (*see* Owen Wilson's tour of Ennui in *The French Dispatch*) / a man in a Jaffa Cakes commerical cycling around England in search of someone who's never tried a Jaffa cake (I can find no evidence confirming my memory of this) / cut to Mr. Bean booking it / Pee-wee being a goof / four friends riding and singing side by side through countryside in *Now and Then* / a night scene where a girl sits on the handlebars or stands on the back of a boy's bike (I still don't know how either position works) / cut to an adult man borrowing a little girl's bike during a chase (I never see someone riding a bike too big for them, always too small) / to Rue biking after Jules through an orange grove in *Euphoria* / to *City of Angels*: above shot of woman biking around Lake Tahoe with arms extending out, then chest opening and head tipped up to the heavens.

(131) *The Mindy Project* series opens with a drunken and heartbroken Mindy fleeing her ex's wedding on a stolen bicycle and toppling into a stranger's swimming pool. Six seasons later, the series finishes with her at her best friend's wedding, borrowing his bike to speed toward love. Her motions appeared to be coming full circle, only she wasn't the same as when she began.

TRICYCLE

VELOCIPEDE

PENTACYCLE

QUADRACYCLE

More is not always better. (132)

(133)   Bicycles typically have 28, 32, or 36 metal spokes per wheel. Lowriders
         have up to 144. More spokes tend to make for a stronger wheel, but
         also more spokes make for a heavier wheel, so the right balance must
         be found. This balance varies depending on the bicycle's environment.
         Maybe it lives on the road and wants light wheels to go fast. Maybe
         it lives on rocky terrain and needs strong wheels to absorb unforeseen
         shocks. One must also consider that not all spokes and wheels are made
         equal. Advancements in rod and rim materials might make for a bike
         with fewer spokes but a stronger rim to compensate. Then there is the
         angled pattern of the spokes that factor into the equation. Ultimately,
         it seems impossible to declare one wheel superior to another . . . more
         spokes superior to fewer . . . no matter how desperately I want there
         to be an objective answer to which wheel is best for me.

(134)   There are many spoke and hub lighting setups available to deck out
         bike wheels. The multicolored varieties create psychedelic patterns
         as the wheels spin. Often these lights are simply spoke beads, like
         barrettes for a bike's hair, which originated with Spokey Dokeys in
         the late '80s. The colorful beads would slide up and down the spokes,
         making a range of clattering sounds that dissipated to silence at faster
         speeds when the beads fled to the rim and were held there by centri-
         petal force. Some glowed in the dark or had reflectors or were neon or
         metallic. They came in the most desirable shapes: lightning bolts and
         butterflies, stars and hearts, and sometimes the heads of trademarked
         mascots of whatever cross-promotion cereal. Spokey Dokeys are like
         time capsules of the much simpler consumerism of my childhood, when
         toys free with food were the.best.thing.ever. and lists to Santa could be
         satisfied with plastic accessories that made music as we played slower,
         faster, solo, together on our bikes.

THE TRADITIONALIST

THE MINIMALIST

THE LUMINARY

THE ACROBAT

THE COMEDIAN

THE SOOTHSAYER

THE DAREDEVIL

THE IDEALIST

THE CRAFTMAKER

THE SCIENTIST

THE GARDENER

THE MAVERICK

(136) It is my thirtieth birthday. A windy leap year end to February. I have
rented a large house on the Long Island Sound for a weekend with
friends. The house is a converted coast guard station on a hill tumbling
down to private beach. The interior is an eclectic bohemian style that
makes us all swoon. We tinker on the piano, sing, read, write, paint,
make rock rainbows, shuffle tarot, take Polaroids, debate unusual wall
art, sink into clawfoot tubs, puzzle, cook and graze and roast marsh-
mallows and talk and laugh loudly and totter over boulders and felled
trees on the pebbled beach and lie under the stars trying to relearn the
sky's lore from youth. Enclosed in one birthday card is a black-and-
white photo with an inscription from my friend explaining that I am
a collector of interesting people just as she is a collector of interesting
old photographs, and this one reminded her of me. A little girl on a
bicycle looking back toward the camera. She is tiny, but I can sense her
frisky smile as she ends her home's yard toward the street. She appears
alone, but clipped in the foreground is another bicycle. I have stood
solitary in front of many roving waters. The love in those days moved
me to these days. I have collected my people, some are here, some are
over there in other cities, countries, continents, but they are all spokes
of love revolving around my wheel called home.

and only when I was moving forward, was I living.

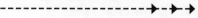

I had thought wheels spinning
on a suspended bicycle was a
stagnation equivalent to death.

But then I fell in love *and life became a spiral.*

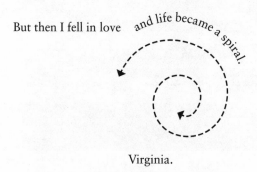

Virginia.

The best human I have ever known.

She got us matching ammonites—like a hypnosis spiral, like two wheels—and for the first time in my life I wanted to spin in one place,

with her.

I

II

Except we'd only ever be a love requited through a sort of amorphous friendship. In her card accompanying our ammonites, Virginia wrote about the ammonite's descendant, the nautilus, and how a nautilus's swirled little cabin is divided into chambers, each growing larger than the last.

> *The first few chambers were filled with only liquid and gas, so that she who lived in the innermost rooms could inflate or deflate the cabin, controlling her submarine to navigate. The nautiluses were constantly adapting, sculpting their ridges and tightening their innermost swirls to make the most of their changing environmental accommodations. They're markers of time, elegantly adaptive symbols of evolution and growth.*

The nautilus is one example of geometry's golden spiral, which grows by a specific ratio with every quarter turn it takes from its starting core. Designers adapt its structure when seeking compositions that evoke natural harmony.

Artist Agnes Denes conceptualized what Earth would look like if shaped like a nautilus shell in her isometric drawing *Map Projections: The Snail* (1976). What if my shell home is the whole world? Denes says she was fascinated by hermit crabs, who move in and out of different shells as they grow. A study conducted by Tufts University in Carrie Bow Cay observed that when a hermit crab stumbles upon a shell that is too big for it, the crab will wait by the shell and be joined by other crabs that come to test it out.[31] They link together in a chain arranged in size from largest to smallest as they wait for a perfectly sized crab to match with the shell. When it does, each preceding crab moves into the shell left vacant in front of them, allowing all the crabs to relocate to the home that's their best fit.

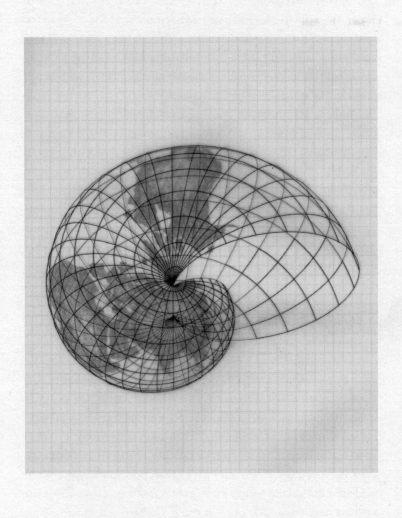

(138) One summer day with our bikes, Virginia and I took the ferry to Sandy Hook Beach, a six-mile barrier spit off the Jersey Shore. The forested bike path running down the center felt like a return to Ottawa's paths, uninterrupted and embedded in green. Having foolishly opted not to bring locks, we torturously dragged our bikes through the sand like some sort of Spartan Death Race before deserting them and walking farther down, past rainbow umbrellas, past fishermen, to the absolute end wisp of land where it was only us and the birds. Faintly etched in the horizon was the New York skyline to the right of the Verrazzano-Narrows Bridge, the foreground was beach and water converging, the midground was Virginia, nose-diving into the waves like a mermaid. We were so removed from the daily grind. Virginia found two dismembered claws of an Atlantic blue crab, mesmerizing in their ombré turquoise joints with red tips that still adeptly bent after being torn from their heart cords.

> I suggested taxidermy. She lullabied *no*.
> We drank them in reverently,
> then she let them go.

Back we rode onto the ferry to Battery Park, then onto a ferry to Red Hook, then off and up through Cobble Hill for evening ice cream. It was more happy than seemed possible for a day to contain. A gamboling jitterbug of biking, swimming, talking, and unspeaking. I wanted to fill my lungs up enough to hold that day in forever, to bend time toward a love I would never own. For now, pain and love deepen in tandem, and I feel the peak of awe all at once with fear. Awe over what a person could mean. Fear of a love that might leave and a future alone, this time neither of which would be my choosing.

Dear Presta Valve,

I hate you.

Screwed so tight, but so ready to explode. You are pretentious with your two valves. Your sensitive outer valve freaks out when I'm too eager or forthright. You're so fussy about which pump you'll hug, it needing to adapt because you can't. I hate how you flatten or fling off when ~~I, and~~ approached.

Don't you want fresh air?
Don't you want to be paired,
like Schrader, in popular usage?

Why can't you stay full
as long as I need??

?

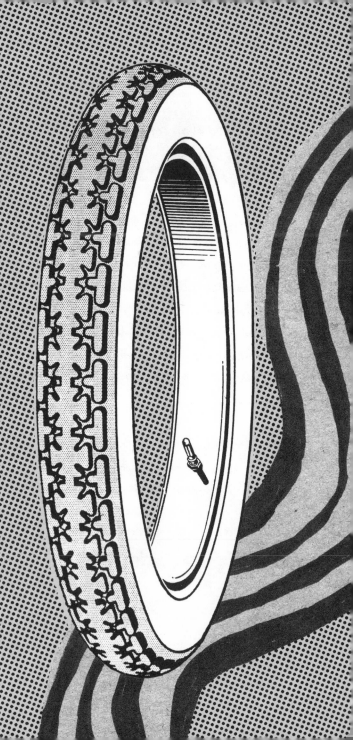

Once a season I am convinced (140)
my inner tubes have a leak. When
neurosis strikes, I take my bike to
whatever shop is nearest. Bike mechanics
will patiently detach the rubber wheels and
submerge my tubes into a bucket of water to
demonstrate no air bubbles can escape. Never
once has a mechanic tried to swindle me into replacing my tubes. Even with assurances, that feeling never
leaves, that feeling that I am not at max inflation.

Online listicles offer many suggestions for how to upcycle bike (141)
inner tubes (one site claims there are one thousand possible reuses):

- create protective waterproof cover for chains, ropes,
  or even bike parts

- weave into a doormat or a chair seat

- cut into a roller stamp, bookmark, headband

- make no-slip house socks or gladiator sandals
  or shoelaces

- replace a laptop key

- sew into a belt, a wallet, earrings, a pencil case

- use as grips on gun handles or juggling sticks

- set them on fire

(142)   In mid-March 2020, New York City began implementing social distancing measures in response to the spread of COVID-19. The mayor encouraged commuters to swap their subway routes for less crowded forms of transport like biking or walking. Suddenly, nationwide sales in commuter and fitness bikes jumped 66 percent over the previous year, leisure bikes 121 percent, children's bikes 59 percent, electric bikes 85 percent, and Citi Bike rides were up 67 percent.[32] Months into Quarantimes, most stores were sold out of affordable bikes, some selling the scarce remains for double. There were waiting lists for bikes as demand outpaced the already disrupted global supply chains of bike parts (because of Asian factory delays due to the virus earlier in the year and US tariffs on China prior to that).

(143)   Pre-pandemic, I biked at most twice a week, mainly to complete errands or travel to meet friends within the borough. As public life shut down, cycling became one of few activities coloring my time. Each ride was hours long, maybe to an international food shop, nature escape, or distinctive architectural era. I rode over bridges up the West and East Sides of Manhattan, crisscrossing its middle. I biked to the shores rimming Brooklyn and Queens and their industrial and cemetery centers. New streets, next-to-usual streets, neighborhoods I'd never been, deeper and wider and more spiraled I went through this city, more thorough, far, and fetched than anyplace else, except maybe back in my teen suburb's self-contained labyrinth. In many ways, the bike inherited an exclusive freedom similar to that time, of being my sole conduit to refuges outside the home.

My housemate was part of that early March bike boom. We put an old (144) housemate's bike on the curb to make room for the new one.

It was gone within the hour.

(145)   Over a two-week period, I stood in line outside the local bike shop for a total of six hours to repair my bike as it wore down from increased trips across the potholed and ratchety city streets. Half the people in line were there for emergency tune-ups, the other half to buy new bikes. First, I needed my front fender adjusted. It was bent and rubbing against my tire from overloading my basket. Then my hubs were nearly ousted from their wheels and required tightening. A brake cord dislodged from its holster. A tire and inner tube were punctured. There was the newly discovered need for a pressurized bike pump, stronger bike lights, a rusted chain to be replaced. I would arrive at the shop an hour before it opened and wait for a couple of hours to be seen by a mechanic. I watched people forced into making quick decisions about which expensive bike to buy in an economy of scarcity. It was becoming a trendy form of activism to support local businesses.

I enjoyed this change to services—small talk with employees, having to be intentional with one's shopping, forced to take recommendations curbside rather than hem-hawing over the "best" product based on critical consumer reviews. I felt a sense of community to these days and an excitement over the few activities that would warrant a field trip from home. International travel was impossible given erratic daily restrictions to visa holders. Airplanes/ports were petri dishes of potential infections. There was so much time now that former nothings became events. I could savor chores, spend half a day making a meal to share and an evening reading, prolong the stages of laundry, dye my overalls with avocado pits, watch a nature documentary, create a home spa day, clean baseboards with a toothbrush, unsubscribe from junk e-mails, spackle and paint the hallway, rearrange furniture, bathe midday, take a walk and use the phone button on my iPhone (much to its confusion, asking if I was sure, if I didn't actually mean to text or FaceTime or communicate with a GIF). My alarm clock app hibernated for over two years. Anxiety evaporated and the mundane became novel. I acclimatized to stillness and relished in what I formerly feared would be declared boring. Maybe external stimuli were just superficial distraction from a more sustainable richness found within. The wisdoms proliferated during the pandemic eerily reinforced the lifestyle I was already learning to lean into. I was grateful for my privileged position in Quarantimes and terrified of what would come next.

Bike dates became a common first and second and third date, since (146) mostly the only people dating in real life were those who were mobile and since inside spots were closed to outsiders. It was odd dovetailing with someone in space before mind. But I also felt a lingua franca with dates who moved through the city at the same velocity, a baseline rapport of being bike people.

One woman I dated for a couple of months. We first met at parks (147) with our bikes, then at her empty apartment. Her dream was to build a city—everything from ideologically to architecturally. I can't think of an ambition that could impress me more. Once as I was returning from her place in Ridgewood, my wheel popped. It was dark, pouring rain, and forty-five minutes before the 8:00 PM curfew that had been imposed during the week following some city looting. I walked two hours home. I had finally stayed somewhere long enough that my inner tube would need replacing, as well as its rubber wheel. I ended things with her soon after. There were many reasons, but . . . I didn't like how after I arrived anemic and breathless to her place, she never offered to help carry my bike up her steep stairs. She'd just watch me heave.

(148) I "heart" any dating profile that makes mention of bicycles, if only
       to kindle my faith in a semiotic universe.

You should leave a comment if

you want to explore! In the kitchen, in the sheets, in the concrete jungle.

We'll get along if

u like to bike around, dig in the dirt, smoke weeds, are a socialist, treasure the outdoors, & take life seriously but not toooo seriously !

Unusual skills

Weaving through NYC traffic on a bike.

I'm looking for

someone who will go camping with me 🏕️...or help me figure out surfing! 🏄 or ride bikes 🚲

One thing I'll never do again

bike while trying to carry a fishing pole

Best travel story

Bicycling from OR to PA on a tandem with my dad, 20 years after my parents' honeymoon (bicycling from OR to PA). Ours can be less ambitious, though.

Together, we could

ride our bikes, sit on a bench in the park, laugh, talk about what we've been reading/listening to and share some odd dreams we've had recently

Typical Sunday

biking around for a sunny spot to read and snack

Together, we could

Good coffee and a crossword, a trip to the library (whenever they reopen 😵) for something new to read or maybe an afternoon bike ride to Riis.

you're a qpoc socialist. you can tell me about space time. you wanna ride bikes to Coney Island and jump in the water.

The sound of the wind while riding a bike in Prospect Park after 10pm

You want to go on a long bike ride. Think Rockaways or Harlem!
Im heading out on a long ride next week and would love a company on train rides :)

you can reference fine art but also come bike camping in the woods 🚲 ⛺ 🌲

filmmaking, IT and cycling 🎥🚴

Washed up child soccer star turned Citi bike connoisseur

Coffee on a cold morning, long runs & bike rides, hiking, falling asleep with a good book

The outdoors, a good book, peanut butter, the revolution, family time, roller disco, bikes, plants

(149)   I started dating a jazz musician named Yuval. Every time we met, one
        or both of us had our bikes. We were Brooklyn bicyclists, for pleasure
        and practicality. She was the nearest I'd come (in the twisted world
        of app dating) to someone I could envision entering a relationship
        with. It felt like we were devotees to the same religion. She made her
        bed upon waking, was punctual, raw, arranged her words in beautiful
        sequences, loved whoopee cushions because they were melodic, remem-
        bered everything I said. I knew if we had taken a compatibility quiz we
        would be highly matched. But maybe she felt too similar to contrast
        me. I wanted compatible difference. I wanted someone to unseat me,
        someone whose unique intelligence eclipsed what I could conceive solo,
        someone more able to marry their internal palace with the external
        world, someone whose world I was desperate to earn membership
        to. I wanted Virginia to be my home. I didn't know if in time I could
        grow to love Yuval as deep but in a form all her own. I didn't know
        when to wait, when to run, whether it was even a decision of which I
        had conscious sway.

To relax in my teens, I made exacting pencil reproductions of photographs from magazines. I would get lost in replicating mostly exuberant women. There is one of Cate Blanchett from a 2004 Annie Leibovitz shoot for *Vogue*. In black and white, Cate is sitting atop a cruiser in a Katharine Hepburn–esque suit. Converse sneakers tucked up on the handlebars. The bike is moving, evidenced by the blurred spokes and ground of what looks like the runway of a private airport. Cate's smiling expression is so animated I can hear laughter when looking at her. I don't think I have ever felt as carefree as this image personifies. I think the closest I've come is when drawing such feelings, having to inhale the photograph's vitality and hold it in my face in order to burnish lead into portraiture. I once wanted to be like this, like a tuft waving in the breeze.

Now those faces are a queasy reminder of an airy womanhood I felt owed that was stolen from me. At this age, I think a different sort of woman would pull me toward mimicry.

Perhaps another Annie Leibovitz portrait, of Susan Sontag (1988), trampled woman.

Some of the largest demonstrations in American history erupted in the (151) summer of 2020. Cyclists were often at the front of marches, some with backpacks indicating they were carriers of free water and first aid. For a couple of the most intense weeks early on, the storefronts in Midtown were boarded up. Fifth, Sixth, and Seventh Avenues were empty of vehicles. I sped through their centers taking no notice of direction or traffic lights, not being able to ride for more than a minute without hitting a side street cordoned off by a police squad. I could see for miles down the empty corridors, the horizon sometimes ending with a crowd of protesters marching in an echoed chant: "We can't breathe." Between the clouded evening sky, concrete skyscrapers, and asphalt streets, the city became film noir scored by the constant helicopters overhead. It was apocalyptic. I was surveying the city at the speed one might skim a future history book detailing the occurrence, flipping its pages of images of Times Square, Union Square, Washington Square, the bridges, the masked white Brooklynites with strollers and cardboard signs filling the streets who not one week ago were told it was their civic duty to stay inside. But instead of reading a retelling framed by a politically slanted newspaper or tweeter or textbook, I was there with my bicycle like a finger running over the ridges defining our age.

Some of the cyclist-led protests echoed the Critical Mass pro-bike (152) movement that began in San Francisco in the 1990s and spread worldwide. Critical Mass is when cyclists routinely gather to ride through the streets in a large enough number that cars must yield to them. Doing so makes a statement about the need for greater road safety and urban planning for bicycles. I joined a well-established bicycle group called NightCAP (Cyclists Against Patriarchy) for trans and nonbinary people and queer and allied cis women. The organizers reliably took turns leading rides every Tuesday night in Brooklyn and arranging weekend meet-ups for other citywide bike activities.

I never was much of a group person, but since living with house-mates, I lust over groups, fantasizing about being a cog in some wheel, participating in an entity that moves with collective force, has webby social dynamics and ongoing events.

From the beginning, it was easy to feel included by NightCAP. For rides, ten to forty people would show up, some regular attendees, some casual riders, some newbies. They had a "no bicycle left behind" policy, with one organizer leading at the front and another trailing at the back. The leader would decide when we would roll through red lights or wait for green. Volunteers blocked intersections so the group could stay together even as traffic lights changed. We were encouraged to take up space and not accommodate cars. This was counterintuitive, but it made for a rollicking ride. Some members would play music from speakers, I would chat with whoever was next to me or zone out in a way that would have been impossible when those same roads were littered with oblivious jaywalkers, car doors swinging open, buses and delivery trucks pulling over, and speeding cars. We would end at a park for evening snacks and socializing. Besides our shared bike threads, everyone there was from different disciplines. Initially, it felt like no substantial meaning could be derived from this anonymous group of small-talking strangers. But soon, I realized that to be part of a group was not to amass a series of one-on-one intimacies with individual members, but to forget the self altogether and expand outward.

In competitive cycling, *to draft* is to trail behind another cyclist in their (153)
slipstream, where one has an aerodynamic advantage and can maintain
higher speeds with greater energy conservation than if confronting the
wind. I am the eldest of four, so this concept is foreign to me.

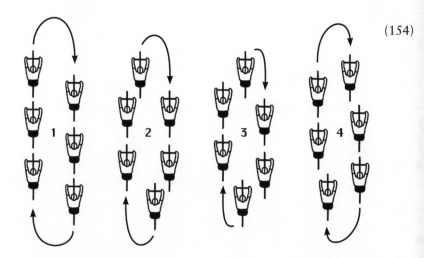

(154)

A team of road racers (called a *peloton*) will draft in various forma-
tions. In a rotating pace line (also termed *Belgian tourniquet*), the
cyclists take turns in the lead position. In smooth revolution, a faster
line of riders will advance as a slower line of riders retreats on the side
where the wind is coming from. The sport is a lot less soloist than it
appears.

Conservationist Terry Tempest Williams defines *dwelling in place* like (155)
continually turning a kaleidoscope on a fixed point so that "infinite
configurations" of a community's complexity are uncloaked.[33] I think
this extends to dwelling in a group, in nature, or even oneself.

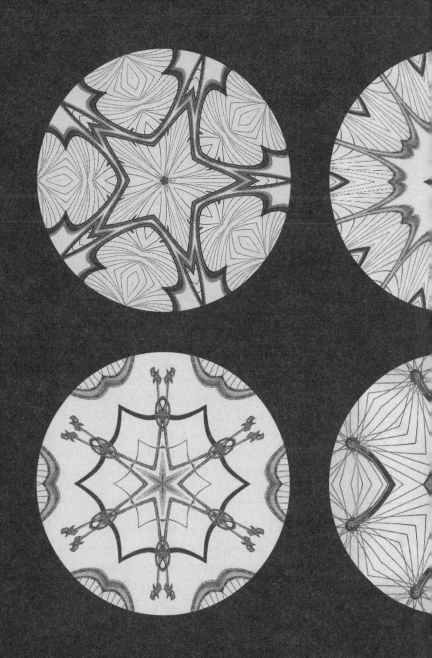

(156)   Sailor sends a raspy voice message from Kashmir saying she is stuck there in COVID lockdown. I earnestly but playfully return a message telling her, "I hope you are not sick. Keep safe. Please don't die, okay?" I learn from a Danusha Laméris poem that "strangers still say 'bless you' / when someone sneezes, a leftover / from the Bubonic plague. 'Don't die,' we are saying."[34] Though our uncertain days stem more from economic distress than toxic air, we still tenderly worry for our loved ones and the Uber driver and the stage artist; the single parent; the bar owner; the healthcare worker; the homeless man; the traumatized baby mouse I found in the sink that morning and released into the garden. Conversations in the media and among friends speculated on what long-term impacts would come out of this protracted quarantine. Some predictions were lofty. I think many were too hopeful for permanent and far-reaching changes. We gradually return to the gluttony and speed of pre-pandemic times. But I think there are smaller residues that will remain—a heightened awareness of injustices, a greater ability to slow, more bike racks, a new overanxious turn of phrase . . . Outside the hardware store where I go to buy mousetraps, I look down at the rack securing my bike.

(157)   After what felt like an impassable conflict with a close friend, anger, anxiety, and despair twined around me so tight I thought I would asphyxiate. I rode my bike along a beach boardwalk, all the while listening to a podcast that coincidentally was on what makes relationships thrive. Relationships work when empathetic communication makes us feel understood . . . While someone is speaking, instead of preparing for a rebuttal, listen and pay attention, not just to what someone is saying but why they might be saying it to you . . . Slow down to really hear the other person's perspective with the deepest desire to understand their truth, their sensitivities, their needs . . . and tend to that core.[35] They were simple words, but the meditative calm brought on by the interfusing of water,[36] cycling's default network mode, and a psychology podcast flooded me with compassion. I became the water, the bike, every person I ever loved, so open and immobilized of thought I wanted to never speak again, only to allow entrance to every truth outside myself. The next morning my friend and I found breakthrough. Now, every time I have a problem I book myself into a free therapy session of cycling along the water listening to a podcast related to my issue.

(158)   The SoulCycle® website says, "Rockstar instructors guide riders through an inspirational, meditative fitness experience that's designed to benefit the body, mind and soul. Set in a dark candlelit room to high-energy music, our riders move in unison as a pack to the beat and follow the signature choreography of the instructors. The experience is tribal. It's primal."[37]

(159)   Pablo Neruda writes in his poem "Ode to Bicycles":
                    only moving / does it have a soul.[38]

(160)   I prefer my rickshaw charm over my bicycle charm because it has wheels that spin.

(161) I try a friend's Peloton. Maybe my joy of cycling will override my hate for instructor-led workouts. Let's pretend you the reader know nothing of Peloton because, like me, you often dwell under a rock where the rays of zeitgeist cannot reach. Peloton is a stationary bike attached to a computer screen that leads the rider through an exercise class. First, I put on specialty clip shoes, because like any coveted product, there are extra accessories required before the product is functional. The shoes click into the pedals, preventing slip-off, but also locking the foot into a mandatory position. Then choose a class. 2000s pop music. The instructor appears on the screen on her Peloton, mirroring mine. She casually mentions she is a former dancer. She is ageless and pretty in a way that I assume is universally pleasant enough to stare at for thirty minutes. We begin pedaling at the cadence and resistance levels that appear on meters on the screen. There is other info on the screen about calories burned, best scores, distances hypothetically traveled. Along one side, comments appear from other Pelotoners participating in the class. It's unclear whether the comments are streaming in real time as we ride, how people are commenting while riding, why anyone needs to be commenting to a group of strangers mid-workout, and what the comments were, since I was too busy trying to decide if I can/want to match my metrics to the screen's to read the comments section. Half the time we lift up off the seat to pedal in a way that is actually running. I hate running so much. Then we sit back down for speedier pedaling as the instructor dances with her upper body while on the seat. She is loving life. She doesn't seem to care that we are watching her be hot while not actually inviting us to be hot with her. The class goes by fast. It abruptly ends. I struggle to detach from the Peloton. My friend comes to unclick my feet from the bike, then from the shoes, because I cannot figure it out. We exit the shed gym that was larger than the journey I had just mentally traversed. My muscle and mind memory are amnesiac. No bike or bicyclist was present for whatever just occurred. Nor any sort of personal decision-making. Whatever has happened was

identical to my feeling toward every workout class I have ever taken. I am vindicated knowing that this part of myself has not changed. That there are categories of things that I used to hate that I reliably still hate.

I visit once New York transplant Farrow, who has returned to her (162) childhood village in Northern California. We kayak, hike, frolic the beaches, and sit in her garden Jacuzzi while cat, dog, horse, and chicken look on. I wish my childhood had been like Farrow's and this village my home. Farrow insists I try her electric bike. 2020 was christened the "Year of the Electric Bike" (Farrow's is technically only her teen mountain bike jankly outfitted with an electric motor). I first refuse. It is not, as American cyclist John Howard writes in *The Cyclist's Companion*, "a curious vehicle whose passenger is also its engine."[39] But Farrow controverts it is more crossbreed than alien, it will assist on hills and back off when I want to motor with muscle. I depart an hour before sunset and zoom through the dense redwoods, along Big River, into the village edging ocean cliffs by the abandoned Highway 1. I know now what is meant by *joyride*. I am a bullet cutting through the blue, heading toward the sun. Here is a new thing that I didn't think I would love and now do, because of friendship. I become an unpaid traveling salesman of electric bikes, I represent all the companies, I have all the facts. Electric bikes are the future. People will cycle farther and for longer than before, they will add cargo trailers for school drop-offs and grocery runs and day trips. Electric bikes are not here to replace bicycles, they are here to replace cars and buses, couches and gym memberships. Please quote me on this.

My childhood "diary" is mostly pages suffocating with lists of things (163)
I wanted to do and have, alongside collages made from cutouts and
stickers. I refused to pick one sticker, I had to have them all. A tiny
bicycle sticker is traffic-jammed by rampant esuriences.

One remote work morning, I decide to go buy a canopy tent so our (164)
house can spend more time on the roof shaded from the sun. There is a
sale at a sporting goods store in Queens. The fastest way is fifty minutes
by bike. The boxed tent fits in my front basket, but tilts like Pisa so
the bike's equilibrium is dangerously off-kilter. The four twenty-pound
weighted feet are split between the basket and my backpack, straining
my back and denting the basket into the front tire. I ride cautiously,
nearly crashing several times as I duck to avoid decapitation by a drone
and swerve around potholes. When I imagine achieving a balanced life,
I try to channel Swiss acrobat Freddy Nock sitting upright on a bicycle
with tires slotted to run over a 1,200-foot tightrope strung up in the
Alps. He holds a long balance pole crosswise to the cable and pedals
steadily, his whole body is obstinately braced as he inches along. In
reality, my attempt at a balanced life looks more like trial biker Kenny
Belaey riding desperate and foolhardy over a sixty-foot slackline, hope
where skill should be, his left leg swinging out and in to counteract the
instability of the task, often his whole body toppling off and jouncing
upside down by an ankle mercifully tethered to the slackline as the
bike swings by a tether above.

Lately, I have noticed kids moving around on two-wheelers missing (165)
pedals and chains—tiny replicas of the bicycle's forefather, the hobby-
horse. These balance bikes are popular alternatives to stabilizer bikes
(those with training wheels). They are better on uneven surfaces, can
be introduced to younger children, assist with developing coordination
and motor skills, are less clunky and heavy, and offer a smoother tran-
sition to cycling. Betterment through erasure. A recent *Nature* study

found that when asked to change or improve upon something, people naturally turn to additive rather than subtractive solutions.[40] Only when scenarios are presented in a form that encourages slow thinking does subtraction enter the equation.

Evolution often connotes complexifying the simple. I am so, so guilty of bloated growth. I.want.everything. I am peckish at best, and at worst, when painted blue, starving for assurances that my life is succulent, or ripening as such. My impulse is to add to my plate, a new project, activity, social interaction. *More is more.* I nod. *No, it's not.* I am stressed, overworked, resentful of my day planner's expansiveness; my back aches, my eyes and brain have stretch marks. But I also have a longer list of good things: people, pride, money, memories, meaning. Everything is so much. I didn't begin with the balance bike. I have never dieted and sustained a regimen of refusal whereby I choose not to swallow, select what only needs to be nibbled, recognize the anaphylaxis caused by that which outsiders insist are vitamins.

(166) In a Hostelbookers.com interview, traveling cyclist Eric Benjamin speaks of his insides containing a barrel of monkeys.[41] When one monkey isn't fed, it goads the other monkeys, wreaking havoc on the psyche. When he cycles, he is feeding his Adventure Monkey to stave off insipidity and depression. I have a similar theory of my insides. When I was twenty-one I got really sick from drug-resistant Indian parasites and ensuing health complications. After a year of exploratory procedures and pills to no avail, Mom and I went to a naturopath. The naturopath first asked about my stress levels. This was before *anxiety* became a buzzword. Mom responded that I was the least stressed person she knew. At the time I haughtily agreed, and for many years her conviction falsified my constitution. I think I meet anxiety with enterprise rather than avoidance, creating an illusion of composure. The naturopath had me complete a Wheel of Life, a self-assessment tool that slices life equally into nine core dimensions. The degree of atten-

tion given to each dimension subconsciously varies. The wheel assists in raising one's awareness of which dimensions are thriving, which are floundering. I was to color in each slice to the level of satisfaction I felt. From then on, I have visualized my life as a whole pie, categorizing my hunger within the dimensions and setting action items accordingly. The pie means there is an upper limit to how much fullness any one dimension can provide, and thus I should place an upper limit to how much energy and expectation are directed to any one dimension. My hunger is not general, my search for satiation requires specification.

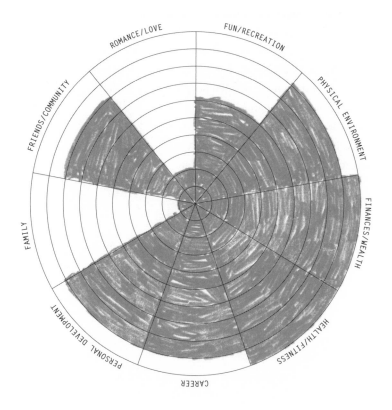

(167) I watched a TEDx Talk with hormone expert Alisa Vitti introducing her hypothesis of cycle-syncing, which, given the historical lag in scientific research on female reproductive health, remains inconclusive. The four phases of a woman's monthly menstrual cycle represent distinct shifts in hormonal ratios. Vitti believes that women can practically adapt their eating, exercise, sex, and productive activities week to week in harmony with the strengths and weaknesses inherent to each phase's ratio. She explains that women are most creative in their follicular phase, have the best communicative abilities and highest energy in the ovulatory phase, are most detail-oriented in the luteal phase, and most in tune with their body in the menstrual phase.[42] It made me reevaluate the time scales of my goals, what needs to be reworked in concert with natural rhythms, how to sensitize myself to the underlying hum.

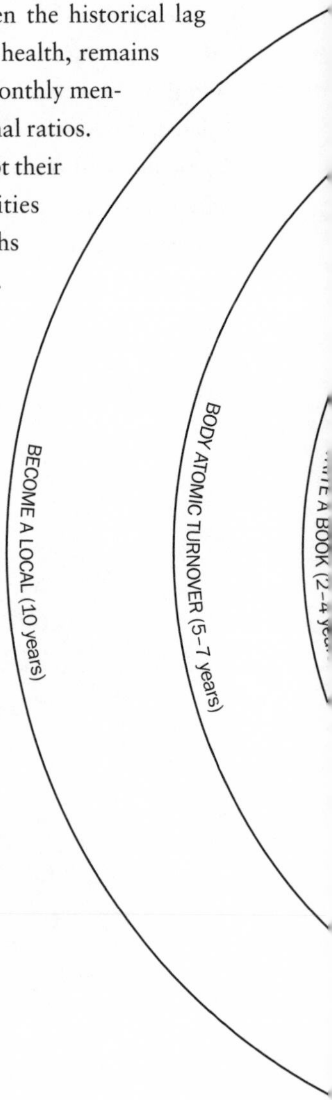

BECOME A LOCAL (10 years)

BODY ATOMIC TURNOVER (5–7 years)

WRITE A BOOK (2–4 years)

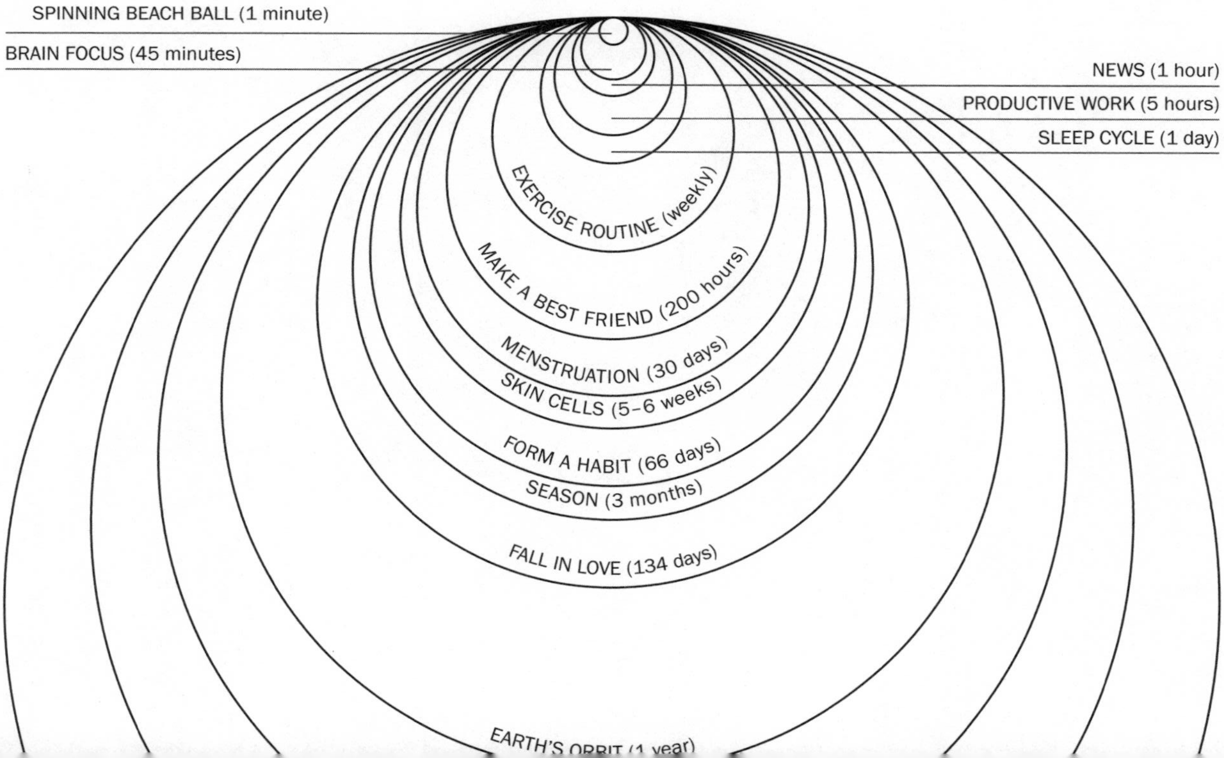

SPINNING BEACH BALL (1 minute)

BRAIN FOCUS (45 minutes)

EARTH'S ORBIT (1 year)

FALL IN LOVE (134 days)

SEASON (3 months)

FORM A HABIT (66 days)

SKIN CELLS (5–6 weeks)

MENSTRUATION (30 days)

MAKE A BEST FRIEND (200 hours)

EXERCISE ROUTINE (weekly)

NEWS (1 hour)

PRODUCTIVE WORK (5 hours)

SLEEP CYCLE (1 day)

R-E-C-Y-C-L-E-D

U-P-C-Y-C-L-E-D

E-P-I-C-Y-C-L-E-D

THINGS THAT ARE NOT "JUST LIKE RIDING A BIKE"	THINGS THAT ARE "JUST LIKE RIDING A BIKE"	(169)
driving a car	navigating the subway	
playing a piano	typing on a keyboard	
completing a crossword puzzle	winning a Scrabble game	
sleeping on an airplane	sleeping in a meeting	
writing checks	cursive writing	
recalling bank passwords	opening combination lock	
communicating French words	conjugating French verbs	
knitting	hair braiding	
removing stains	mixing colors	
dancing	Hula-Hooping	
remembering punch lines	remembering poems	
putting in a contact lens	putting in a menstrual cup	
stretching pizza dough	folding a Cootie Catcher	
threading a sewing machine	tying shoelaces	
ending things	starting things	
diving	swimming	
sex	loving someone	

(170)   Riding in so many diverse conditions has made me overconfident. I approach each bicycle like an old friend, mounting the borrowed and rented as if we have known each other for years. Then not a minute later, as I am a few pumps in, I am reminded that not all bikes are the same. Each has her quirks, the used ones also have defects, and even if the ratio of saddle to ground and saddle to handlebar are a perfect match, there will be unexpected twists that will make me instantly miss some other bike's bike-iness that I took for granted—the shape of the seat, the reactiveness of the brakes, the tires' shock absorption, the weight of the frame, the logic of the gears, my angles against hers. Disgruntled, I will carry on, and the bike will tame me to its version of discomfited freedom. Later retrospectively, all I will remember is how lovely those bike times were.

(171)   If I were to break a bike in two, which half would I take? The front commands, the back fuels. Do I want to be the leader or the workhorse? Is it my choice? Can't I be like the bike, defined by both?

(172)   Holed up working in his Manhattan studio until late, my friend told me his bike would often be missing different parts when he left at night. Once, he rode home without a bike seat. Once, his bike was stolen. He said it hurt his feelings.

A classic New York street scene. (173)

Does the frame suffer phantom limb syndrome? Where do those parts end up? Do they feel homesick? Have they found a new home with which to belong?

A friend[43] told me about a dream he had "in which someone stole a (174) number of parts off of [his] road bike, but then replaced them with parts from a child's bike: the pedals, the seat, the stem, and one of the wheels."

Aging is like this—as experiences expose more of the world, my annexed wisdoms shrink back into naiveties relative to the ever-expanding whole.

(175) A year into Quarantimes, most of my city friends had relocated to other parts of the country, my housemates went on to solo living, Virginia left for school upstate. The grief was more than I thought possible. The loss of a network of friends was not my choice. I was the one who did the leaving, I didn't get left. I wasn't ready for a homelessness. I desperately wanted out of my reality, but there wasn't another place that made sense.

I had applied and been accepted to a master's program somewhere else, but turned it down. I would have been running away, not toward something. Younger me would have said yes. Younger me always said yes to the novel and kinetic, believing it superior for growth and prestige. But there wasn't a right decision. There never is. And I am learning that to stay in one's place is also an action.

One day in Washington Square Park, where I was collecting a dining room chair for my new apartment from a Craigslist post, I came upon a man named José selling old bicycles from his van. I went straight toward a kelly-green Peugeot Mixte. I had already decided to replace my Schwinn Suburban, researching used, electric, and new bicycles for months. After a year of more intensive riding, my needs had changed. I wanted something lighter for when I brought it on the train for out-of-city trips. I wanted something slimmer to slide in my under-stoop closet. I wanted something with sturdier rear storage capability.

I returned to José over several weeks as he retrofitted the Mixte to my liking. He added collapsible baskets on either side of a rack, which tripled my transport capacity, affixing them with nuts taken from my old Schwinn that he was rehoming. He advised on pressure levels I should maintain in the tires given my exact weight (which he guessed down to the pound). He told me it was rare to find a Peugeot with all its original stickers and crest intact. A sticker read "RECORD DU MONDE"—*world record*, or, as I like to think of it as my *recorder of world*. Like how *life cycle* and *cycle life* are becoming synonymous to me.

New bicycle purchases only ever coincided with disrepair, growth spurts, big moves—abandonment forced upon me—and were always replaced with the cheapest option. The Mixte wasn't the cheapest option (it cost $300, my most expensive bike to date), but otherwise I suppose this time was no different, only I was the one in disrepair, the growth spurt internal, the big move two neighborhoods over.

As a Tree that seeks t  (176)
a
p
r
o
o
t
e
d
n
e
s
s,

I have begun to identify my discomfort as a thirty-something single New Yorker as *root-bound*. I cycle the same concrete routes, hardly demarcated by natural seasons, as people – – – – – – – ➤ come · · ┐ then leave ◄ – ┘ for more porous lands.

There is so little left that I wish to do in this pot for one. I grow round and

(177)   Some notes on boredom. Søren Kierkegaard called boredom both the root of all evil and the initiator of motion. To combat it, he proposed the "Rotation Method": as with agriculture, fertility demands continual change in cultivation methods and crop types grown; enjoyment could be maximized through arbitrary experiences upon which one applies imaginative reflection.[44]

Millennial vernacular might label boredom *the blahs*, *the blues*, *the scaries*. The feeling is *Groundhog Day*, that I'm simply reliving the same day, every day, until I die. The feeling is *I am spinning my wheels*, that this never-ending day is one of the busyness of securing a livelihood, a busyness that does not accumulate from day to day but rather resets itself before the next dawn.

John Martin Fischer explores philosophical debates around the extreme case of whether living would still be desirable if it never-ended and there was unlimited time to fill. Fischer suggests that immortality does not need to guarantee inoculation from boredom or pain to be ultimately worthwhile: "Why think that because a life is *unending*, it must be *uniformly* pleasing in order to be on balance attractive?" Sure, he writes, there are many forms of pleasure, the *self-exhausting* and the *repeatable types*, some even "endlessly fascinating" in their "*reliability*, *density*, and[/or] *infinite extensibility*," but it would be obtuse to presume that one's relationship to those pleasures will endure, because as time progresses, so does one's relationship to the future, and one's aims, values, and affinities given acquired wisdoms and reckonings.[45]

Maybe my current "boredom" powers a propeller, and I am nearing the apex of a rotation out of busyness into the life of an ascetic or an apiarist, or something.

The brain seems to favor recurring routes . . . the pain cycle, the circular fear-avoidance model, the cognitive/emotive loop. Something happens, it makes the brain feel a certain way, then think a certain way, then behave a certain way, and a pathway is dug. A similar thing arises and we begin to feel, think, and behave along that trodden pathway, and it gets paved. A therapist suggests I try elongating my segments between feeling and thinking, as if my brain were a rubber band ball with elastics I could tug between my thumb and index finger. It sort of is *elastic*, a *plastic*. The pathways paved in early life are superhighways for processing, only to be reconstituted in adulthood through habitual focus on emotionally stimulating activity. The vagueness is intimidating, but internet lists on exercises for rewiring neural pathways are essentially about learning and doing challenging new things until they become easy and known. I assume, though the lists did not say, that once such a thing is conquered, it should be replaced with another curious challenge. I assume, though my therapist did not say, that in my case the conquest is irrelevant, it is the challenge that slows my sprint. Humility toward the untrodden topography ahead stalls this path between feeling and thinking.

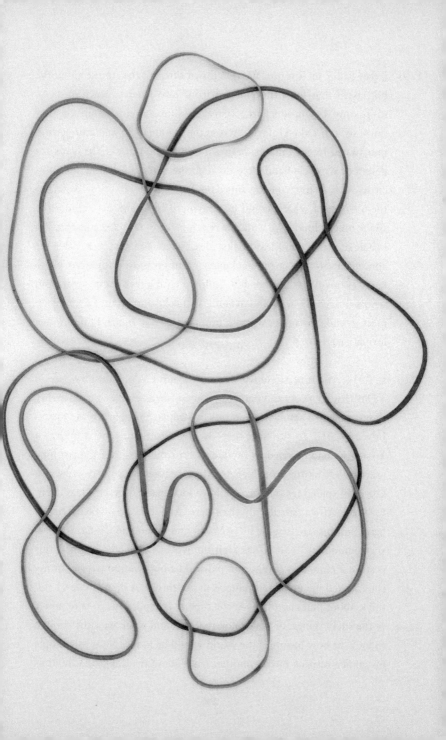

(179)   I visit Sailor in Toronto. We ride down through the Annex along the bike path that hugs the Harbourfront into Cherry Beach and out to Tommy Thompson Park, a straggly human-made peninsula that ejects us into Lake Ontario. Across the lagoons, the miniature city is punctuated by the tall upside-down exclamation mark. The trails are deserted. We cycle hands-free through the marshy forest in autumn's citrus hues, singing "Here Comes the Sun," to the tip of the park. On the horizon of what I could be convinced is ocean, there comes the sun through clouds. We walk the beach made of recycled construction rubble of water-smoothed bricks, tiles, concrete blocks, and rocks. We concentrate too long on stacking sculptures and deciding which to keep. I convulse from the chill. Sailor silently takes off her scarf and wraps it over my head and around my neck, zipping my jacket up to meet its end. She smiles warmth into me. *Let's go home.* I think, some love is easy.

(180)   In 2011, YouTube streamed the crowdsourced documentary *Life in a Day*. Ridley Scott and company edited the assemblage from eighty thousand video submissions taken by ordinary people worldwide on July 24, 2010. In the film, there is a Korean man named Okhwan Yoon who had traveled by bicycle to 190 countries over the last nine years. He is sitting in a Nepali café watching this fly struggle in a saucer of spilled tea. He says, "I have seen many different sizes of fly. In North Africa, smaller fly than here. And Turkey, smaller fly than here. But this size is same fly in Korea and Japan and China. So I feel very emotional."[46] Yoon has seen the world's wonders, but it is this pest on a plate that brings him pause. His observation panged at my soul, welled my eyes, and lumped in my throat. A decade later, I still think about that clip often. At the time, it reminded me to take notice of the small things, of a meaning that is found when we slow enough to look, of how beautiful the world would be to me. Now, this simple insignificant speck buzzes another truth about the things that bind us

to one another, not identical things, but same enough; everywhere we are, but also, there is felt a subtle variousness through which we seek to thread a unified whole.

Mom survives off flipping houses. She moves into a dump in some (181) outskirts, labors on visionary renovations and decorative hacks, then sells it at a profit. She says she is looking for her forever home, but each house is pronounced a flip by move-in day. I don't know what would become of Mom if forever arrived. I grew up in a very specific type of suburb and have since generically run from all similarly categorized settings. I suspect rural living would feel like a demotion, an externalization of my inner introvert that would silently kill me. But the urban is overstimulating; it baits my hidden hustler, taunts me with noncommittal community. I'm afraid of seeking out a quiet place to settle and turning into Mom, secluded and listless. I'm afraid that this thought is what keeps me running from where I belong.

The Wizard of Oz ends with Dorothy revealing the film's moral of (182) "there's no place like home," saying "If I ever go looking for my heart's desire again, I won't look any further than my own backyard, because if it isn't there, I never really lost it to begin with." I began like Dorothy, dreaming of the world out there. Then a tornado came and swirled me into it and I am still swirling, circumvoluting along a vortex street. I can't tell anymore if I am swirling up toward Oz or back down to Kansas. Unlike Dorothy, if home is my moral, my home is not the one I was born into, nor is it the one I would have freely chosen.

What does it feel like for home to be where you want to be and also where you're supposed to be, where others are supposed to be too, where everything feels exactly right? When I catch a whiff of this feeling I try not to breathe for fear of disturbing it. Like a house of cards collapsed by a sigh. When I was a tween, I taped the playing cards together, extra wide and four stories high, to build a permanent house display on my bedside table. The tape would eventually dry and peel, the cards left slumped and tacky. Is there a place where this feeling dwells not in a moment but in a lifetime? I watch others enter and exit the feeling freely. Mine feels distant, a horizon line that keeps moving as I move. Why can't I want what I already have? Why can't things stay enough? Why can't the people who feel enough stay with me?

(183) Biking around Ottawa after a decade of living abroad, I am struck by a historical locality that was lying dormant in my hippocampus. I intuit the views before turning corners. There are layers to my coordinates. I know not only this path I ride but also where it connects, the greenbelt and farmlands yonder, the smell of these damp leaves after an autumn rain—it is a capacious peripersonal space, a positional belonging that spans a me that, though having changed over cellularly several times since, was me, ten years ago, twenty years ago, thirty years ago, here. In *Imaginary Homelands*, Salman Rushdie rejoices migration for its "hybridity, impurity, intermingling, the transformation that comes of new and unexpected combinations of human beings, cultures, ideas, politics, movies, songs."[47] In *Staying Put*, Scott Russell Sanders challenges Rushdie: "If you are not yourself *placed*, then you wander the world like a sightseer, a collector of sensations, with no gauge for measuring what you see." What is a life that is settled in a place, yet supple to transformation? Sanders argues that "all there is to see can be seen from anywhere" if one stays long enough that the stillness becomes a holy center.[48] Perhaps there is no forever right place, self-evident and beckoning before arrival. Perhaps a place's rightness is a bilateral entente between me and a place together defining home for a time.

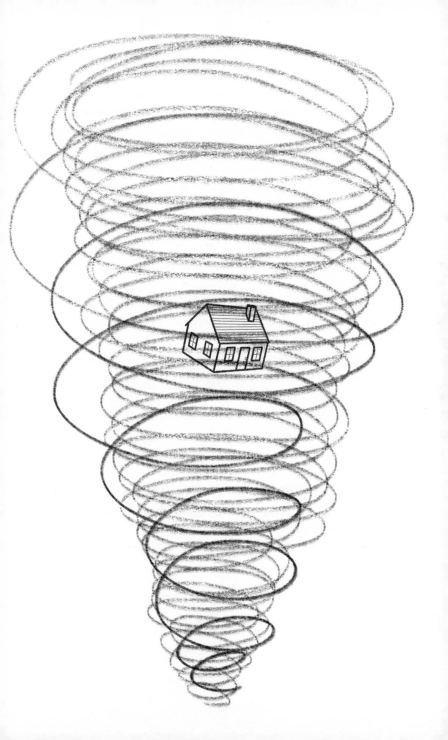

BIKE RIDES to-do

(184)

- [ ] Copenhagen, Denmark   [x] AMSTERDAM
- [ ] Buenos Aires, Argentina   [ ] Lakeshore Trail, Chicago
- [x] Old Delhi, India — [ ] KERALA
- [ ] Yangshuo, China   [ ] Island hopping → Croatia
- [ ] Ella, Sri Lanka   [ ] RIO DE JANEIRO, BRAZIL
- [ ] Cambodia → Angor Wat to Siem Reap
- [ ] SARK, CHANNEL ISLANDS
- [ ] Nantucket   [ ] Kingdom Trails, Vermont
- [ ] Dingle Peninsula, Ireland
- [ ] Otago Peninsula, New Zealand
- [x] New York Beaches   [ ] Golden Triangle, Rockies
- [ ] CABOT TRAIL, Nova Scotia   [ ] Whitehorse – single track
- [ ] Challenger Seven Park Loop, Texas
- [ ] Bermuda Railway Trail   ~~RAILWAY TRAIL~~
- [x] THAILAND + VIETNAM   [ ] Queenstown Trail, New Zealand
- [x] Brighton Beach (UK)   [ ] Queen Charlotte Track, NZ
- [ ] Uluru, Australia   [ ] Vieques Island, Puerto Rico
- [ ] Arnold Arboretum, Boston
- [x] Fort Lauderdale (visiting grandmother)
- [ ] Turku Archipelago, Finland
- [ ] PORTLAND, OREGON   [ ] BAINBRIDGE ISLAND, Seattle
- [ ] CAPE COD – Bikepack   [x] Marina del Rey, Santa Monica
- [ ] FRIENDSHIP HIGHWAY, Tibet   [ ] Traveler's Rest, South Carolina

☐ San Juan Islands, Washington

☒ Bologna   ☐ Tuscany, Italy   ☐ Berlin

☐ Ubud, Bali, Indonesia   ☐ Balboa Park, San Diego

☐ Montreal   ☐ GASPÉ PENINSULA

☐ OLD CROTON AQUEDUCT TRAIL, NEW YORK

☒ Northern California, Highway 1 Ocean

☐ The Great Ocean Road, Australia ☐ Carretara Austral,

☐ EASTER ISLAND, CHILE   ☒ Highlands, Nairobi ᶜᴴᴵᴸᴱ

☐ Song-kul Lake, Kyrgyzstan

☐ Hiawatha Trail, Idaho ☐ Ketchum, Idaho

☐ VINTAR GORGE, SLOVENIA ☒ TRANSYLVANIA

☐ Grand Teton National Park, US

☒ Over Golden Gate Bridge, SF, CA

☐ Lofoten Islands, Norway ☐ Gulf State Park Pier,
                                          Alabama
☐ Land's End to Bude, UK

☐ 4 Rivers Path, South Korea ☐ Ljubljana, SLOVENIA

☐ Hauraki Rail Trail, New Zealand   ☐ EUGENE, OR

☐ Historic Columbia River Highway State TRAIL, oregon

☐ Nishiseto Expressway, Japan   ☐ Banff Legacy
                                         Trail
☐ Stanley Park Seawall, Vancouver

☐   ☐

☐   ☐

☐   ☐

☐   ☐

☐   ☐

☐   ☐

The story of my life doesn't exist. Does not exist. There's never any center to it. No path, no line. There are great spaces where you pretend there used to be someone, but it's not true, there was no one. The story of one small part of my youth I've already written, more or less—I mean, enough to give a glimpse of it. Of this part, I mean, the part about the crossing of the river. What I'm doing now is both different and the same. Before, I spoke of clear periods, those on which the light fell. Now I'm talking about the hidden stretches of that same youth, of certain facts, feelings, events that I bur

that drove me t

was still someth

writing is nothi

writing isn't, al

a quest for vani

not, each time, al

some inexpressibl

advertisement. Bu

that all options a

more barriers, th

where to hide, to

unseemliness is n

stop thinking abou

Now I see that

fifteen, I already

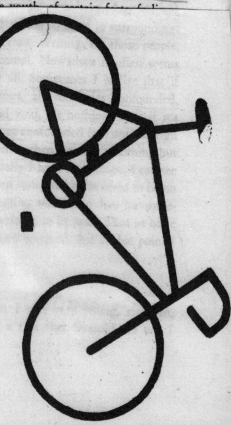

LEFT: The bookmark tucked in my copy of *The Lover* by Marguerite Duras.

The bicycle is said to be a symbol of freedom. But I don't think this (186) book is about freedom. Maybe a little: the freedom to individuate, to free myself from mediocrity and an unhealthy family, to be master of my fate, to go at my desired speed. But I *am* free. Yet, there remains a deep yearning in me. I thought I would stay in New York forever, but now six years have passed, and I am starting to daydream about moving on. This book might be about searching for people who can house enough wonder and love and home to quell a looming melancholy. It might be about realizing that exists only in pathways I must keep cycling through.

Valeria Luiselli writes, "Riding a bicycle is one of the few street activities (187) that can still be thought of as an end in itself . . . [T]hat person—who has discovered cycling to be an occupation with no interest in ultimate outcomes—knows he possesses a strange freedom."[49] Novelist Leslie Jamison ponders a certain brand of motivation wherein "significance dwells in concentric circles of labor around an empty center—commitment to an impetus that resists fixity or labels. The persistence of 'why' is the point: the elusive horizon of an unanswerable question."[50]

We learn first the thing, second our relationship to it. Then third? My "why" persists. I know motion, these cyclettes I am doodling . . . as a form of distraction . . . a form of art . . . to fill the margins because the center is not mine to write.

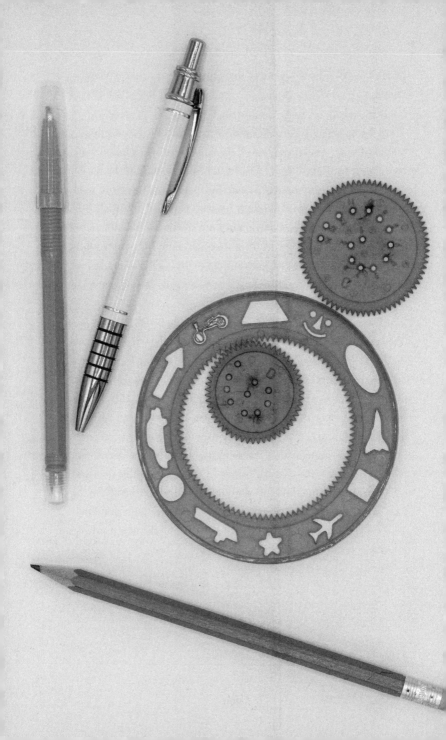

If you're a kid in 1908, maybe you have the Marvelous Wondergraph; (188) in 1967, an Art-Gizmo harmonograph; in 1982, a Cyclograph; in 2018, a Hypnograph; or any time after 1965, like myself, a Spirograph. These drawing machines were a mystery to me, circles that appeared to move circularly, but never completing a circle, no matter how many times the small gear moved around the inner or outer radius of the large gear. So fractionally errant from circularity, the winding roulette curves of hypotrochoids, epitrochoids, epicycloids, hypocycloids, rosettes, and star bursts made infinite portholes into sacred geometries.

As I enter these portholes—portals—I feel like an early explorer. Some- (189) one who felt their way through unmarked lands. Someone swallowed by blizzard or darkness or desert zone so vast and enduring across horizons that they ceased to be able to track from which direction they came, how far they'd traveled, and where their intentions should lie. I imagine it is in these moments of most profound lostness that an explorer must declare her existence as signpost enough for what's next. I am here, whether cycling through an unknown territory or spiraling around a somewhere home, all about in these places and people, I am here.

NOTES

1. All the names of people mentioned from my life have been changed, partially for privacy's sake, but mostly for fun.

2. Girl Scouts of the United States of America. *Scouting for Girls: Official Handbook of the Girl Scouts.* 3rd. ed. Girl Scouts, 1922, p. 507.

3. Gordon, Ann D. (ed.). *The Selected Papers of Elizabeth Cady Stanton and Susan B. Anthony.* Vol. 6, *An Awful Hush, 1895–1906.* Rutgers University Press, 2013, p. 34.

4. Reid, Carlton. *Roads Were Not Built for Cars: How Cyclists Were the First to Push for Good Roads & Became the Pioneers of Motoring.* Island Press, 2015.

5. Colville, William Wilberforce Juvenal. *Dashed Against The Rock: A Romance of the Coming Age.* Colby & Rich, 1894.

6. Pond, Dale. "Keely." Sympathetic Vibratory Physics. Pond Science Institute, last modified, 21 March 2022, svpwiki.com/Keely.

7. Simanek, Donald E. "The Keely Motor Company." Hoaxes, 2013, lockhaven. edu/~dsimanek/museum/keely/keely.htm.

8. Simanek, Donald E. "Why won't my perpetual motion machine work?" The Museum of Unworkable Devices, last modified August 2020, lockhaven. edu/~dsimanek/museum/themes/whynot.htm.

9. Tanenhaus, Sam. "On Being Noam Chomsky." *New York Times,* 6 November 2016.

10. Brickman, Philip, and Donald T. Campbell. "Hedonic Relativism and Planning the Good Society." In *Adaptation-Level Theory.* Ed. M. H. Appley. Academic Press, 1971, pp. 287–305.

11. Lyubomirsky, Sonja. *The How of Happiness: A New Approach to Getting the Life You Want.* Penguin, 2007.

12. Debatty, Régine. "Interview with Michel de Broin." *We Make Money Not Art* (blog), 26 June 2012, we-make-money-not-art.com/michel_de_broin/.

13. Doob, Penelope Reed. *The Idea of the Labyrinth: From Classical Antiquity through the Middle Ages.* Cornell University Press, 2019.

14. Užkoraitis, Edgaras (Cyclist enthusiast). "If you were a bicycle what part would you be?" *Quora*, 7 January 2017. https://www.quora.com/If-you-were-a-bicycle-what-part-would-you-be.

15. Koeppel, Dan. "Riding China's Flying Pigeon Bicycle." *Bicycling*, 30 April 2010, bicycling.com/rides/a20021347/bicycling-in-china/.

16. Thomas, Neil. "The Rise, Fall, and Restoration of the Kingdom of Bicycles." MacroPolo, Paulson Institute, 24 October 2018, macropolo.org/analysis/the-rise-fall-and-restoration-of-the-kingdom-of-bicycles/.

17. Blumberg, Arnold. "Pedal Power—Bicycles in Wartime Vietnam." HistoryNet, 6 July 2012, historynet.com/pedal-power-bicycles-in-wartime-vietnam/.

18. Edwards, Betty. *Drawing on the Right Side of the Brain.* J. P. Tarcher, 1979.

19. Delves, Joseph. "Around the world in 80 days with Mark Beaumont." *Cyclist*, 8 December 2017, cyclist.co.uk/in-depth/3858/around-the-world-in-80-days-with-mark-beaumont.

20. Berenstain, Stan, and Jan Berenstain. *The Bike Lesson.* Beginner Books, 1964.

21. Aciman, André. *Alibis: Essays on Elsewhere.* Farrar, Straus and Giroux, 2011, p. 48.

22. Cole, Teju. *Known and Strange Things.* Random House, 2016, p. 67.

23. Olson, Charles. *Proprioception.* Four Seasons Foundation, 1965.

24. Debord, Guy. *La société du spectacle.* Buchet-Chastel, 1967.

25. Nietzsche, Friedrich. *The Gay Science.* Vintage Books, 1974, p. 273.

26. Ibid., p. 14.

27. Lima, Manuel. *The Book of Circles: Visualizing Spheres of Knowledge.* Princeton Architectural Press, 2017.

28. Odell, Jenny. *How to Do Nothing: Resisting the Attention Economy.* Melville House, 2020 (paperback), p. 7.

29. Jung, Carl Gustav. *The Archetypes and the Collective Unconscious.* 2nd ed. Routledge, 2014, p. 388.

30. Mastretta, Catalina Aguilar, director. *Everybody Loves Somebody.* Pantelion Films, 2017. 1 hr., 42 min.

31. Jabr, Ferris. "On a Tiny Caribbean Island, Hermit Crabs Form Sophisticated Social Networks." *Scientific American*, 5 June 2012, scientificamerican.com/article/vacancy-hermit-crab-social-networks/.

32. Goldbaum, Christina. "Pandemic Has Americans Snapping Up Bicycles, Creating a Shortage." *New York Times*, 19 May 2020.

33. Williams, Terry Tempest. *Erosion: Essays of Undoing*. Sarah Crichton Books / Farrar, Straus and Giroux, 2019, p. 305.

34. Laméris, Danusha. "Small Kindnesses." 2019, danushalameris.com/poems.html.

35. Vedantam, Shankar (host). "What Makes Relationships Thrive." *Hidden Brain* (podcast), 17 January 2022, hiddenbrain.org/podcast/what-makes-relationships-thrive/.

36. Nichols, Wallace J. *Blue Mind*. Little, Brown, 2014.

37. This passage was taken from soul-cycle.com in 2020 but has since been replaced with this description of the SoulCycle® experience: "SoulCycle is an immersive and intense full-body workout. Our legendary instructors guide you through class—helping you lose yourself in the ride, the music, the experience. We ride to the beat, whip our towels in the air, and occasionally scream out our favorite lyrics at the top of our lungs. It's an epic cardio party on a bike and you're about to be obsessed."

38. Neruda, Pablo. *Selected Odes of Pablo Neruda*. University of California Press, 2011, pp. 284–85.

39. Howard, John, Albert C. Gross, and Christian Paul. *The Cyclist's Companion*. Stephen Greene Press, 1987.

40. Converse, Benjamin, et al. "We instinctively add on new features and fixes. Why don't we subtract instead?" *Washington Post*, 15 April 2021, washingtonpost.com/outlook/2021/04/15/psychology-innovation-subtraction-addition/.

41. Benjamin, Eric. "Love Cycling? Interview with a Professional Travelling Cyclist." Hostelbookers, 16 August 2011, hostelbookers.com/blog/travel/love-cycling/.

42. "Loving your lady parts as a path to success, power & global change: Alisa Vitti at TEDxFiDiWomen." YouTube, uploaded by Tedx Talks, 6 December 2011, youtube.com/watch?v=9vKRj9yV8pl.

43. "Friend" in this case refers to Book*hug's editor for *Cyclettes*, Malcolm Sutton.

44. Kierkegaard, Søren. *Either/Or: A Fragment of Life.* Penguin, 2004.

45. Fischer, John Martin. "Why immortality is not so bad." *International Journal of Philosophical Studies*, vol. 2, no. 2, 1994, pp. 257–70.

46. "Life In A Day 2010 Film." YouTube, uploaded by Life in a Day, 21 January 2011, youtube.com/watch?v=JaFVr_cJJIY&t=1818s.

47. Rushdie, Salman. *Imaginary Homelands: Essays and Criticism, 1981–1991.* Penguin / Granta Books, 1992, p. 394.

48. Sanders, Scott Russell. *Staying Put: Making a Home in a Restless World.* Beacon Press, 1993, pp. 114–16.

49. Luiselli, Valeria. *Sidewalks.* Coffee House Press, 2014, p. 36.

50. Jamison, Leslie. *The Empathy Exams.* Graywolf Press, 2014, p. 107.

ILLUSTRATIONS

Page 6: Card given to me by my grandmother on my first birthday.

Pages 26–27: Screenshot of Google Map, printed and drawn on.

Page 38 (Clock Diagram): Abbott, Allan V., and David Gordon Wilson. *Human-Powered Vehicles.* Human Kinetics, 1995.

Pages 42–43: Scott, Robert Pittis. *Cycling Art, Energy and Locomotion: A Series of Remarks on the Development of Bicycles, Tricycles, and Man-Motor Carriages.* J. B. Lippincott, 1889, p. 274.

Page 53: Personal rendering of Michel de Broin's *Entrelacement* (2001). The original, made in asphalt and paint, is located off a bike path by Canal Lachine in Montreal.

Page 67: Backside of a sandpaper scrap, imported from China but collected from a market in Harar, Ethiopia.

Page 86: An election poster torn from a wall in Bangladesh. Large text reads "cycle," small text reads "vote for the cycle party," though my Bengali friend said that it was probably for a local commissioner position wherein the symbols on election posters are random and the "cycle party" probably has nothing to do with green politics or bicycles.

Pages 90–91: GPS art made with the Strava app and uploaded by users to strav.art. TOP LEFT: Pomeroy, David. "ROLLING DOWN COLUMBIA PIKE." Arlington, USA, 2014. BOTTOM LEFT: Álvarez Pons, David. "NIGHT RIDE." Barcelona, Spain, 2021. TOP RIGHT: alex.on.bike. "✂ - - - 🏍 🕊 - - - 🦟 - - - 😜 - - -." Van der Valk Resort Linstow, Germany, 2017. BOTTOM RIGHT: Vdp, Charles. "ADMIT IT LOOKS LIKE A CYCLIST." Brussels, Belgium, 2020.

Page 103: Black-and-white Shutterstock adaptation of "Rotating Snakes" (2003) by Japanese psychologist Akiyoshi Kitaoka. Motion is even more pronounced in the full-color version.

Page 113: *Uitgezonderd* is Dutch for "except for."

Page 155: Denes, Agnes. *Isometric Systems in Isotropic Space—Map Projections*. Visual Studies Workshop Press, 1979, p. 274. Image 61 from web.archive.org/web/20150304045458/http://www.artistsbooksonline.org/works/mpjs.xml.

Page 167: Pencil reproduction of Cate Blanchett photographed by Annie Leibovitz for American *Vogue*. Condé Nast, December 2004.

Page 168: Pencil reproduction of Susan Sontag photographed by Annie Leibovitz in *A Photographer's Life, 1990–2005*. Jonathan Cape, 2006.

Page 204: Duras, Marguerite. *The Lover*. Pantheon Books, Inc., 1997, p. 8.

ACKNOWLEDGMENTS

In order of appearance: Many thanks to my parents for not letting me grow up into an adult who never learned to ride a bike. To Samantha Hunt for confirming in her workshop on "Surrounding the Ghost" that a chalk outline could be the body of a story. To Lindsay Wilson for always being my first and fastest reader. To Abigail Frank for convincing me *Cyclettes* was both beautiful AND saleable. To the Publishing Twins for serving as my hype girls. To Andrew Faulkner at Invisible Publishing for early support. To Mina Hamedi for advice and future collaborations. To Chris Heiser and the entire Unnamed Press team for believing in this project and trusting my vision. To Nancy Tan for adding back as many hyphens as she took away. To Jay and Hazel Millar at Book*hug Press for carving out space for indie books in Canada, my strange cover designs, and now, this. To Malcolm Sutton for asking existential questions in the margins. To NightCAP for things only found in a pack. To Brian Lemus for being my Quarantimes biking buddy. To Adela Wagner for Aftertimes spun on and off our bikes. And to Sanba Bicycle Shop for doing nearly-free, quick repairs whenever I need.